CW00594831

Beer is Best

John Watney

Beer is Best

A HISTORY OF BEER

PETER OWEN · LONDON

ISBN 0 7206 0333 1

All Rights Reserved. No part of this book
may be reproduced, in any form or by any means,
without the prior permission of the publisher.

PETER OWEN LIMITED
20 Holland Park Avenue London W11 3QU

First British Commonwealth edition 1974
© John Watney 1974

Printed in Great Britain by
Daedalus Press Stoke Ferry King's Lynn Norfolk

Contents

Illustrations

Illustrations are reproduced by courtesy of the following: the Brewers' Society (3, 5, 6, 9); John Courage Ltd (1); Watney Mann Ltd (7, 8); Joshua Tetley and Son Ltd (10, 11, 13); Scottish and Newcastle Breweries Ltd (12).

Illustrations on the title page and on p. 65 are from a series drawn by Mervyn Peake for the Brewers' Society and are reproduced by permission.

I am greatly indebted to Peter Evans of the Brewers' Society for his help and encouragement in writing this book.

J.W.

Part One

Down the Ancestral Throat

Chapter One

'*Hek*,' said the Ancient Egyptian petulantly.

Immediately his retainer brought him a beaker of beer.

This drink would not have tasted like any kind of modern beer, for there were no hops in Egypt to give the fermented barley the distinctive bitter taste of beer. It would have been more like sweet ale, also made from barley but without the addition of hops. But the method used five thousand years ago, of moulding barley into a kind of malt and then fermenting it, has not basically changed since. The means of brewing, not brewing itself, has become more sophisticated.

Hek, even then, was a very popular drink. *Hek* shops were to be found everywhere in Egypt. They became so numerous, indeed, that about four thousand years ago the authorities came to the conclusion that there were too many of them and tried to close them down, making the drinking of *hek* illegal.

This is the first recorded example of prohibition.

Hek was also used as a medicine, a tonic for those whose strength needed building up, or so a medical manual of the time would indicate. It is mentioned in the *Book of the Dead,* and there was even a god, Osiris, allocated to the drink, according to Herodotus, that not very reliable historian. He added that Osiris taught the Egyptians how to brew *hek* because they had no vineyards, and thus could not make wine.

But the Ancient Egyptians knew how to make wine long before Herodotus wrote his controversial history. Both *hek* and wine were probably made simultaneously. According to Aeschylus, it was not considered a very good drink. The Pharaohs would drink wine, their subjects *hek*.

Hek continued to be drunk in Egypt for centuries, and existed

11

until comparatively modern times, under the slightly altered name
of *hemki*. Even at the end of the last century, a traveller on the Nile
recorded that he saw the crew of a ship make an intoxicating liquor
from barley bread and water. The name of this concoction was, the
traveller declared, *boozer*.

The Jews of the Old Testament also knew how to make a drink
from barley. They probably brought the recipe out of Egypt with
them at the time of the Exodus. Some historians believe that the
Hebrew word *sicera* covers the brewing of all non-grape alcohol
whether from corn, barley or honey, although in Tyndale's Bible
the word is translated as 'sydyr' or cider. *Sicera* was also supposed
to protect its drinkers from leprosy. The Jews remained free from
the disease during their captivity in Babylon because, it is said,
they drank *sicera*.

The Ancient Greeks, who made the first and best of wines, did
not think much of the various brews made from barley. Only the
Thracians to the north seem to have preferred their home-brewed
drinks to wine. Xenophon mentions a malt drink brewed by villagers in Armenia in 401 BC. Despite the responsibility of leading his
ten thousand Greeks through hostile territory from Mesopotamia
to the Black Sea where safety lay with the Greek ships, he had time
to observe the customs of many of the places he traversed during
the extraordinary march that followed Cyrus's disastrous defeat.

This particular village was situated deep in snow-covered
mountains. All the dwellings were underground, their entrances
being holes in the ground that resembled wells. Ladders led down
to the living quarters. In every home there was always a large bowl
of brewed malt, filled to the brim. Hollow reeds of various lengths
lay beside the bowl, and when anyone wanted a drink they picked
up a reed, dipped it into the bowl and sucked vigorously. The
liquor, Xenophon records, was very strong but not unpleasant,
once one got used to it. People in the Khanns district of Armenia
still live in the same kind of underground houses today, but the
art of brewing seems to have been lost.

It was not however until barley found its way to northern Europe, probably by way of the inquisitive trading Phoenicians, the
first to send their ships out of the Mediterranean, that the drink
began to be brewed in greater quantities. It has always been more
popular in northern than in southern countries.

It was the Danes who first called the drink they brewed from barley, ale, or *öl*, meaning oil. The name slowly took over from all the various local names along the north German coast and in Britain.

The Ancient Britons drank *metheglin* and cider. *Metheglin* was not, as its name seems to indicate, a kind of tranquillizer, but mead. It was made from wild honey found in hollow trees and was drunk by the more primitive nomadic tribesmen. The honey could be scooped up during hunting trips and brewed immediately around the camp fire. It was essentially an 'instant' drink, needing no special preparation or preservation.

Cider was also a drink that suited the needs of wandering tribes. The small hard apples grew abundantly on the stunted crab-apple trees. Again, it was just a question, when the men were out hunting, of picking the quantities they needed.

Ale had been introduced into the British Isles just before the Roman Conquest. But even so, it was restricted to the more advanced tribes of the South-East. They had ceased to be nomadic and had settled down on the land as cultivators, thus being able to sow the barley that was needed for making the new, fashionable drink from northern Europe. The Romans did not think much of ale, and even less of the *metheglin* they found as they pushed northwards. They considered that all British home-grown brews were undrinkable. It seems that only the local oysters received Roman approval; empty British oyster shells from sumptuous Roman feasts can still be found wherever Romans lived.

Ale seems to have reached Ireland about the same time as St Patrick, for 'suppers with ale' are mentioned in the *Senchus Mor*, the ancient law book of Ireland composed about AD 430. An Irish chief was expected to have in his house three sacks and two casks. The sacks contained malt, salt and charcoal; the casks, milk and ale. It is not revealed who was to drink the milk and who the ale, but it is not too difficult to guess.

In Wales, ale was a luxury. Mead was the common drink for centuries both before and after the Roman Conquest. The ale was kept in casks that, according to an old ruling, must be 'so capacious as to serve the King and one of his counsellors for a bathing tub.' There were two kinds of ale in Wales. One was common ale, the other spiced. Spiced ale was twice as expensive as common ale and four times as expensive as mead. Wine was completely unknown to the Welsh, although there is mention of a vineyard at Maenarper, near Pembroke in South Wales, about a century after the Roman Conquest, but this was probably planted by an exiled Roman, homesick for his native land.

There is no record of ale having reached Scotland at the time of the Roman Conquest, or in the subsequent years of Roman occupation. But then neither did the Romans. They were content to build Hadrian's Wall and let the Picts and Scots sit on the other side, drinking their own peculiar mixtures.

By the time the Roman Empire ended, and the legions were recalled to the defence of Rome itself, ale was a fairly well-established drink, particularly along the northern coastline of Europe and the wilder islands out to sea. There are occasional mentions of it being drunk even as far south as Spain, but on the whole wherever the grape could grow it ousted barley as the basis of a country's ordinary drink.

The grape frontier runs along the River Loire in France, then to the north of the Champagne country, over the Vosges and thus into Germany. This 'line' divided the wine drinkers from the ale drinkers even at the time of the Roman Empire. There were incursions on both sides. The Romans marched north with their casks of wine, merchants headed south with samples of barbaric ales; but, at least as far as drink was concerned, the grape line divided Europe more effectively than any geographical frontiers.

Chapter Two

The Anglo-Saxons were serious and dedicated drinkers. Their speciality was the feast. The great hall would be cleared; the guests would assemble; the lady of the house would arrive and pour out the drinks. There would be a great variety : wine, mead, cider (sometimes called *æppelwin*) and *piment*, a mixture of wine, honey, and spices. Ale, however, seems to have 'borne the brunt in drinck-ing' and soon after the arrival of the Anglo-Saxons became the national drink of the country.

In *Aelfric's Colloquy*, a young man is asked what he drinks. He replies, 'Ale, if I have it, water if I have it not.' Asked why he does not drink wine, he replies, 'I am not so rich that I can buy me wine,' and adds that it is a drink for 'the elders and the wise.'

The Anglo-Saxon religion was full of drinking. Paradise was described as a great hall where the departed gathered, not to play harps like their Christian rivals, but to drink copious and endless draughts of delicious ale. Even when the Anglo-Saxons were finally converted to Christianity, they did not entirely give up their hopes of an ale-drinking hereafter, and half expected their casks to follow them. However, just in case there was nothing but harps ahead of them, they put in an extra amount of ale drinking whilst they were here.

The Saxons and Danes were convivial people. There was nothing they liked better than getting together into guilds or frater-nities, in order to help each other in their commercial or other affairs, and also to have excuses for drinking bouts. If a member defaulted in some way, he was immediately fined – in malt. The malt was then turned into ale, and another evening out quickly arranged. Cries of *'Wacht heil'* and *'Drinc heil'* were shouted across the table as the goblets were lifted.

15

The brewing of the ale itself was the responsibility of the women of the household. Indeed Alreck, King of Hordoland, very sensibly chose Geirhild for his queen because she was so good at brewing ale.

In the late Saxon period, ale was sometimes called *woet,* from the Saxon *swatan.* Although the word was soon lost to most of the British Isles, it remained in Scotland for many years, reaching down even to Robert Burns who wrote : 'It gars the swats gae glibber doun.'

This ancient ale was extremely strong. One tankard was often enough to send a Saxon warrior or his Danish rival reeling off into the night, a song on his lips. Old ale was fed to the pigs, in order to give their bacon the required taste.

But the Saxons did not restrict the use of ale to merry-making, the composition of songs and the flavouring of bacon. It was considered a cure for almost every kind of illness. Clear, not sweetened ale was the magic potion. Ale mixed with various herbs such as bishopwort and fen-mint was a certain cure for fever. As the devil was considered to be behind many illnesses, particularly those of a neurotic kind, many of the remedies consisted of a mixture of herbs, religious incantations and ale, presumably to make the mixture palatable. As bitter pills, in a later age, were covered with sugar to make them edible, so in Saxon days, sweet herbs were mixed with strong ale to help them down.

A popular remedy against 'fiend-sickness' was to mix a number of herbs into clear ale, add garlic and holy water and, after the singing of seven masses, make the patient drink the remedy out of an inverted church bell. It was then guaranteed that even the most fiendish of devils would take to his heels and leave the possessed body calm and healthy again. And if you suffered from stiff knee-joints you only had to rub in a mixture of woodwax, hedge-rife and ale to be mobile again. Nor was the medical use of ale restricted to human beings. According to an Anglo-Saxon veterinary surgeon, nothing cheered a sheep up more than a little new ale poured quickly down its throat.

Ale was frequently used as a means of paying toll, rent or debts. In 852 a certain Wulfred rented land from the Abbot of Medeshampstede, as Peterborough was then called, for the payment of two tuns of pure ale.

The Church, from its earliest days, was strongly attached to ale. Regulations were strictly laid down : there was to be no drinking in the church itself, but a daily portion of ale was allocated to each priest. To monks, living in the carefully regulated conditions of monasteries, a daily portion of ale was part of the accepted and normal diet, just as, in the wine-growing areas of France today, a flagon of wine is part of the daily diet of Benedictine monks. Many monasteries brewed their own ale rather than relying on the local brewer. A monk was appointed cellarer. His only, and most important function was to taste the ale as it was made, and declare when it was fit for drinking. This was a position of considerable responsibility; prayers were said for him, as much to help him resist the temptation of drinking too much, as for his soul. Despite the prayers of their bretheren, however, many cellarers had to be put to bed in a more exuberant mood than one might expect from a holy man.

These erring brothers were not dealt with severely, as it was realized that by their calling they were exposed to more than usual hazards. They were allowed to sleep off the effects of their devotion, while their companions prayed that at the next tasting the cellarer's fortitude would be stronger. Other monks were not let off so lightly. St Gildas the Wise, as early as the sixth century, decreed that any monk whose speech got too thick through an excess of ale, and was thereby unable to sing the evening psalms, was to go without his supper. There were strict rules about drunkenness, although there was a distinction between getting drunk through ignorance and doing so deliberately. The novice, tricked into drinking too much ale, had to do fifteen days' penance, the hardened toper, forty.

The churchman's jurisdiction sometimes extended beyond the priesthood. The seventh Archbishop of Canterbury, Theodore, who held the post for twenty-five years from 668 to 693 decreed that if a Christian layman drank too much, he faced a fifteen-day penance. Heathens appear to have been let off free.

Sometimes kings also tried, like the Ancient Egyptians before them, to restrict the drinking of their subjects. King Edgar, under St Dunstan's not too inspired influence, decreed that there was to be only one alehouse per hamlet. Notches were to be marked on drinking horns, and topers were only allowed to drink down to a certain notch. This early form of rationing was an extremely unpopular innovation.

But although there were occasional and local restrictions on drinking in Saxon times, ale had taken such a hold on the population that it was by far the most important drink of the various states in the British Isles. Indeed, apart from a few very remote places where the earlier drinks such as mead were still produced, ale was the national drink.

There were no breweries, large or small. Brewing was undertaken by one member of each small closely-knit community. The brewer, like the butcher, the baker and the candlestick maker, was an accepted figure in the hierarchy of the village. Though considered essential, his position did not rank very high. Certainly nowhere near that of the blacksmith or the armourer.

The brewer himself would either grow the barley he needed or, in most cases, arrange the necessary purchases. He would see that the ingredients were added in the correct amounts, but the actual brewing itself would be the responsibility of his wife. The word ale-wife was used by the Saxons to describe these brewing ladies.

Although brewing was not a hazardous occupation, there were in early Saxon times penalties and punishments for bad brewing. The most popular was to seat the offender in a ducking-seat and dip him or her in the village pond.

Even during the great Viking invasions of the ninth century, when all that was left to King Alfred was Wessex, that land comprising the south of England up to the Thames-Severn line, ale was drunk by both attackers and defenders. It was, perhaps, the only thing these enemies had in common.

In December 877, just as Alfred was about to sit down to his Christmas dinner and, no doubt, to a beaker of ale, at Chippenham, his temporary capital, the Danes attacked, and he was forced to flee in disguise to Athelney (it was here that he was reputed to have been scolded by a housewife for letting her cakes burn), where he stayed until he was able to muster his forces and defeat the Danes at Ethandune in 878.

So, for the long period of Saxon prominence, ale was the main drink of the country. All sections of the population, kings, abbots, knights, yeomen and villeins drank it. The Saxons were an easygoing people, except when roused or attacked, and were quite happy to spend their days carousing at their favourite feasts, and pouring good strong ale down their throats.

The brewer, with his wife and family, lived in a small house on the outskirts of the hamlet. To draw attention to himself and to guide people to his alehouse he would stick a pole above his door and tie a bush or branch to it. These early inn signs became as familiar as the blacksmith's anvil and the wheelwright's wheel. Very soon, people got into the habit of gathering at the house with the green branch hanging above the door. Travellers arriving at the hamlets would make for it too. It became a recognized meeting place for the community.

The pub was born.

Chapter Three

In 1066 William the Conqueror landed near Hastings and defeated Harold in battle. Quickly moving inland, he partitioned the country up among his supporters and, in order to keep the mass of the Saxon population subservient, built huge castles at strategic points. Britain became a two-nation country. On top was the Establishment consisting of the Norman conquerors in their castles, the majority of abbots whose allegiance had always been towards Rome rather than their former Saxon overlords, and those members of the Saxon hierarchy who had accepted the inevitable and collaborated with the invaders. Below them was the mass of the peasantry. There were sporadic attempts at resistance, but once Harold and the earls had been replaced, there were no real leaders left. The one exception was Robin Hood, believed now to have been a Saxon earl, who fled to Sherwood Forest and raised there a group of resistance fighters. It is significant that in all the tales of his deeds, he invariably robbed the rich, i.e., the conquering Normans, to give to the poor, i.e., the beaten Saxons. He was particularly hard on those abbots who had grown rich by accepting Norman rule.

Apart from Robin Hood, the Saxons soon accepted the reality of the Norman occupation, and life went on as before; but among the changes that the Normans brought about was a little publicized, but fundamental one : in drinking habits.

The Normans, like the Romans before them, brought their own eating and drinking standards. Soon even the language showed these differences. A live sheep still kept its Saxon name, but when it was cooked and appeared on the Norman table, it became *mouton* (mutton). The same occurred with ox and *boeuf* (beef) chicken and *poulet* (pullet) and many others.

Wine was the natural drink of the conquerors. They imported it from France. Soon it was the drink of the overlords and the abbots. Though ale continued to be drunk by the mass of Saxon peasants, it lost its universal appeal. Whereas before, wine had been a luxury, now it had its social context. And ale became the people's drink.

There can be little doubt that it was ale rather than wine that Robin Hood and his 'merry' men drank, along with the rest of the Saxon population. Many of the alehouses adopted Robin Hood or Little John as their favourite heroes. Couplets were composed in their honour and declaimed at get-togethers:

> To Gentlemen and Yeomen good,
> Come in and drink with Robin Hood,
> If Robin Hood is not at home,
> Come in and drink with Little John.

Though the abbots drank wine, the priests and particularly the monks continued the old habit of drinking ale. Drinking, unlike love-making, was, and still is, never considered a sin by the Roman Catholic Church. One has to wait until the arrival of John Wesley and the Nonconformists to have drinking declared a sin.

In the twelfth century, as in Saxon times, the Church's concern was merely to contain drinking at a reasonable level. Thus in 1102, Anselm decreed that priests were not allowed to take part in peg-drinking bouts. These bouts had developed unexpectedly from King Edgar's earlier decree that drinking horns were to be marked by pegs or notches. Instead of restricting drinking however, it had encouraged competition. He who could take his opponent 'down a peg' quickest was the winner.

Crafty citizens spent much time then, as today, discovering ways to get round tiresome laws and regulations. A thirteenth-century attempt at this became known as Scot-ales. Common Law required that a certain amount of tax was levied on all ale consumed (the habit of taxing the drinker of alcohol is as old as drink itself), but Common Law held jurisdiction only over cultivated or open spaces of land. Much of the country was covered by dense forests, and here one could drink 'scot-free' ale.

Sometimes, however, even scot-ale was not as free as it could be. To protect drinkers from attacks from both man and beast,

foresters would set up 'safe' alehouses in forest clearings, where for
a modest fee, the good inhabitants of the local hamlets could get
their scot-free ale. As these fees were a good deal less than the tax
under Common Law, the people took to trecking to the local forest
in ever greater numbers.

The authorities, under the disguise of the Church, stepped in to
prevent this serious loss of revenue. In 1256, Giles of Bridport,
Bishop of Salisbury, forbade the drinking of scot-ales. All the
priests under his jurisdiction were told to see that his instructions
were carried out, with dire threats of what would happen to them
in the next world if they ignored the Bishop's order. His efforts,
however, were not quite as effective as he might have wished; for
the problem was that most of his priests also frequented the cheerful scot-ale house in the forests.

Another custom that was frequently abused was that of bede-ale.
Bede-ale was based on a generous conception: if an honest man
lost money through no fault of his own, his friends were allowed, by
law, to drink him back to prosperity. A certain percentage of the
money paid for the drinks was handed over to the unfortunate man
whose fortunes had 'decayed'. The logical conclusion was, of
course, that if you really wanted to help your 'decayed' friend, you
had to get blind drunk in the process. So many kind-hearted people
dedicated themselves to saving 'decayed' friends that the custom
had to be discontinued.

Yet the echo of the bede-ale custom remained for many years,
and drinking oneself out of debt was for long considered a typically
British solution to a world-wide problem.

In 1348 and 1349 the Black Death ravaged Europe. Whole
communities were utterly destroyed and the casualty-rate was un-
precedented. Half the people of England were killed within a few
months; it took two centuries before the population reached the
level it had been before the arrival of this scourge from Asia. It even
stopped the apparently never-ending Hundred Years War for a
time, through sheer lack of man-power. Even farming almost came
to a halt: crops rotted in the fields and cattle roamed unattended
across the open countryside. The Black Death attacked indiscrim-
inately at all strata of society. So many priests died that the Pope
decreed that laymen could give the last sacraments to the dying.

The Black Death had a curious side-effect on the drinking of ale.

Because of the scarcity of men, labourers could and did demand high wages. This led to an increase in the independence of the labourer, who would, as described in William Langland's *Piers Plowman*, no longer accept half-penny ale but only the 'Beste and the Brouneste that Brewesters sullen.'

At this time, the 'Beste and Brouneste' of ale was often brewed in London, using the then clear and sparkling waters of the Thames. So popular with the brewers were the waters of a conduit built at Cheapside, that the city authorities had to restrict its use for commercial purposes, as the people who lived there complained that they had not enough for domestic use.

London-brewed ale of the 1370s is mentioned in Chaucer's *Canterbury Tales*. The Cook praises a 'pot of London ale' while the Miller blames his drunkenness on the large amount of 'ale of Southwerk' which he has imbibed. In the Miller's Tale of the two Cambridge students who spend the night eating goose and drinking ale with the miller of Trumpington, Chaucer records:

> This miller hath so wisely bibbed ale,
> That as an hors he snorteth in his slepe.

But not all writers of the time were so fond of their ale. John Taylor, writing nearly three centuries later (in 1637) records that Henry D'Avranches had this to say of ale:

> For muddy, foggy, fulsome, puddle, stinking,
> For all of these, Ale is the onely drinking.

D'Avranches, Taylor claimed, was the only writer he had ever read to say anything nasty about ale, but then D'Avranches was an abstainer and drank nothing but water. Taylor records with glee that, because of this unhealthy water-drinking habit, D'Avranches 'fell into such convulsions and lethargick diseases' that he was almost given up as dead. However an astute doctor found the cure just in time: it was a concentrated course of ale drinking. D'Avranches recovered not only physically but mentally as well, and lived to praise ale, in what Taylor, with fearful punning, calls a 'most Aleoquent and Alaborate' way.

It was not only in poetry that ale was mentioned. A very popular miracle or morality play of the fourteenth century concerned the 'tapstere' or ale-wife of Chester. These miracle plays, or Misteries as they were also called, were performed by touring repertory companies and their purpose was to instruct as well as to entertain.

The play describes the descent of Christ into hell with the object of rescuing all the sinners tormented there. All are eventually redeemed, except one : the 'tapstere' of Chester. Her crimes are so terrible that even Christ cannot save her. She admits that she has not only brewed bad ale all her life, but has short-measured her customers as well. She is immediately carted off by attendant demons and flung back, still carrying her false-measure jug, into the mouth of hell. A carving showing the miserable ale-wife, naked but for an elegant hat, being thrown back into hell, can be found in Ludlow Church.

The Sad Fate of a Mediæval Ale-wife.

Chapter Four

In the early part of the sixteenth century a decisive change occurred in the drinking habits of the British Isles. In 1524 or thereabouts a large number of Flemish immigrants, fleeing from persecutions in the Lowlands, arrived in the East and South-East of England. They were people from all kinds of trades and professions, and they brought their knowledge and expertise to their new country. Among the immigrants were a number of hop-growers. They brought their hop plants with them and began planting them in small fields which they acquired, particularly in Kent.

These hop plants were the female kind, known as *Humulus lupulus*. The Romans called them *Lupus Salictarius,* from the fact that hop plants were as destructive to the willows, near which they liked to grow, as wolves were to sheep.

For centuries the hop was somewhat shunned because of its bitter taste, but it is known that it was used by many early civilizations to flavour the somewhat unexciting ale, in addition to other seasoning herbs. It is possible that the hop plant found its way to the British Isles before the sixteenth century, but it never seriously challenged the supremacy of the traditional strong ale of the country.

By 1520, however, the Flemish hop-growers had managed, by experimenting and careful blending, to produce what they called '*bierre*'. This drink was basically ale flavoured with the bitter juice of the hop plants.

It quickly caught on along the north European coast; and when the Flemish immigrants arrived in Kent, they tried to interest the local brewers in taking up the new *bierre*. Many would not touch this new-fangled, foreign brew, declaring that the ale that was good enough for their forefathers was good enough for them. However, a few brewers, either more adventurous or perhaps genuinely believing that the new drink was better than the old, began to buy hops from these Flemish farmers, mixing them with their ales, and selling them to their customers.

Slowly *bierre,* or beer as the lazier local inhabitants called it, began to become more popular. It spread out of the immediate area of Kent to London, and then all over the country.

Oddly, the word 'beer' had been known from Anglo-Saxon times, and for a while it had contended with the Danish word *öl* for supremacy. But by the tenth century its usage had declined so much that it had come to mean a sweet non-alcoholic drink. As if overcome by shame at such a degradation, the word disappeared altogether from Britain around the year 1000, to return some five centuries later, no longer sweet, but bitter from the addition of Flemish hops. Its return was celebrated in the old couplet :

> Hops and turkeys, carp and beer
> Came into England all in one year.

Although the basic principles of making ale and beer are the same, it is not enough to merely add hops to the ale that has already been brewed; the hop-adding is an integral part of the brewing process.

Yet even before the new drink had gained general favour, unscrupulous brewers, wishing to capitalize on the growing craze but too lazy to go through the whole brewing process, took a short-cut. Flavouring their ale with hops, they offered it to the public as beer. Offenders, if caught, were immediately fined as much as five shillings (25p) for this offence.

Not everybody, however, welcomed the arrival of beer. Its popularity was slow in developing. The British have always taken their time to accept novelties, even in that age when discoveries were bringing new kinds of food, trees and flowers almost every year. Many thought they might be poisoned by the bitter hops which took away the comparative sweetness of their accustomed ale.

Even Henry VIII, who normally accepted any novelty eagerly, instructed the Royal Brewer of Eltham in 1530 not to use hops. Many brewers were taken to court by their own alesmen for supplying a foreign drink made with hops instead of the good British ale that was ordered.

Writers took up the popular cause and condemned the new drink. Andrew Boorde in his medical book *Dyetary,* published in 1542, says with stern patriotism that 'Ale for an Englysshe man is a natural drinke,' while beer is the natural drink for a Dutchman. He goes on to warn potential drinkers that it is dangerous to health, and can indeed kill those troubled with gall-stones and other 'colyckes'. He also warns that even if it does not kill you, it makes you fat and inflates the belly, as, he adds with virtuous but devastating logic, 'it doth appere by the Dutche men's faces and belyyes.'

With such terrible warnings against it, it is no wonder that it took many years for the new drink to become firmly established.

Even towards the end of the century, after nearly eighty years of existence, beer had hardly reached Scotland, but this may have been partly because of the difficulty of getting the necessary hops up to the Scottish brewers.

A hundred years after its introduction, controversy continued. In *Wine, Beer, Ale and Tobacco* published in 1630, the various drinks are personified. Thus Beer in introducing himself to Wine makes the modest pun on his name : 'Beere leave, sir' (By your leave, sir). In the subsequent conversation between the three drinks the relationship between them and the public is clearly stated :

Wine : I, generous Wine am for the Court.
Beer : The Citie call for Beere.
Ale : But Ale, bonnie Ale, like a lord of the soile,
       In the country shall domineere.

Wine continued to be the court or upper-class drink, as it had been ever since the arrival of William the Conqueror. The more novelty-seeking town-dwellers would be the first to take to the new beer; while the country people, traditionally conservative, would stick to the old drink, ale.

The songwriters were not slow to express local opinions. A popular air of the time began :

And in very deed, the hops but a weed
Brought over 'gainst law, and here set to sale,
Would the law were removed, and no more beer brewed,
But all good men betake them to a pot of good ale.

The song goes on to recount that beer is a killer and, using again the much-loved device of a pun, will bring the drinker to his bier. It ends with the statement that the first man to brew beer was hanged, and found his 'Beer far more bitter than Ale'.

The first mention of hops in the Statute Books occurs during the reign of Edward VI (1547-1553) when it was decreed that all arable land should be dug up except 'land set with saffron and hops'. Hop-searchers were appointed; their duty was to detect defective hops and burn them. On 10 September, 1551, thirty-one sacks of unwholesome hops were burnt at Finsbury Field by order of the Lord Mayor of London.

By the end of the sixteenth century the popularity of hops was reflected by their price. From 6s 8d (33½p) a hundredweight in 1524, it had risen to £4 10s 6d (£4.52½p) a hundredweight by 1591, and this was during a period when prices had remained relatively static.

With the increasing popularity of beer, the question of producing efficient hop gardens became important.

The early Flemish immigrants grew their hops wherever they could, but by 1574 pamphlets were being produced giving expert advice on how best to grow the plant. Reynolde Scot wrote a book called *A Perfite Platforme of a Hoppe Garden*. It was published in that year 'at the Signe of the Starre' in Paternoster Row, and was dedicated to William Lovelace of Bethersden in Kent, an ancestor of the poet Richard Lovelace.

Scot says that he has heard that Lovelace wishes to build a hop garden, and would be happy to give him all the help he can. He is all for improving the standard of English hops. There has been far too much dependence on foreign hops, he declares, and there is no reason why all the hops required for the brewing trade cannot be home-grown. For although the Flemish immigrants had introduced the plant to England, their compatriots who remained in Flanders had not been slow to take advantage of the new market, and had flooded England with foreign hops.

Scot's pamphlet is extremely precise, and the methods of planting he advocates have hardly changed since. Six years later, Thomas Tusser in his *Five Hundred Points of Good Husbandry* gives a great deal of practical advice in the form of four-line, rhyming stanzas.

Scot and Tusser's efforts must have been successful, for by 1608 an act was passed forbidding the importation of bad hops. But although Walter Blith speaks, in 1643, of hops as being a national commodity, most of the hops required still came from abroad. It was not, in fact, until 1690, in order to encourage home-grown hops, that a duty of twenty shillings a hundredweight was imposed on imported hops.

By then, beer was definitely established once and for all as the national drink of the country. From henceforth beer becomes the generic term for all barley-malt drinks, whether hop-flavoured or not. Though ale continued to be drunk for many years, and can still be found under various labels, it is today, to most people, just another kind of beer, and not a drink in its own right.

The introduction and acceptance of hops in the brewing process was the last great innovation in the history of beer manufacture. Since the seventeenth century the process has seen only the changes introduced with automation and new technology, in other respects the 'mystery of brewing' has remained unchanged. Let us then consider the 'mystery' as it is practised today.

Barley, the basis of all beer brewing, is a ubiquitous plant. It can grow on top of mountains, and even in quasi-desert conditions. Only the barley grain itself is used. When it has been threshed and sieved, it is placed into steeping tanks filled with water. It is then left to soak for two or three days, according to the humidity of the atmosphere.

When it has absorbed about 60 per cent of its weight in water, it is taken out of the steeping tanks and spread out on the malthouse floor. The floor is generally made of hard-baked clay, cement or slate. The grain will already have started to germinate, and is known as green malt.

During this period, various chemical changes take place. The malthouse staff watches the proceedings carefully, and the grain is turned over at least once a day. Wooden rakes are used for this, although in modern brewhouses, the work is done mechanically. Temperatures are kept at about 55°F to 60°F. Germination can be slowed down by spreading the grain, and accelerated by heaping it up.

After about a fortnight, the green malt is moved for drying to the kiln, where it is heated to temperatures of between 110°F and

210°F to dry it. The speed with which it is dried will determine the
kind of beer that is finally brewed. Thus, mild beers are produced
by the malt being dried over wood fires at very high temperatures.
Sometimes, the malt is roasted in cylinders at temperatures as high
as 400°F. Small proportions of these roasted black malts are used
in the production of strong ales and stout.

When the drying process is completed, the malt is stored in bins
for at least five or six weeks. At the end of that time it is ready for
use.

It is carefully sieved and run through a magnetic field to remove
all impurities, including metal objects. It is then cracked, or ground
in a mill.

It is at this stage that small quantities of wheat malt (made in
much the same way as barley malt) are added. Sometimes, rice and
maize are also added. Sugar is an important element at this stage.
This is where the art of the brewer comes in, for the proportion of
these added materials will largely determine the strength, flavour
and even the colour of the beer. This mixture is known as the grist.

The grist is now transferred to a mash-tun, a large tank lagged to retain the heat. To the grist, which has been previously warmed, is added water, or liquor as it is called, at 152°F. This is the infusion method. The whole mass is stirred for twenty minutes and then allowed to stand for two hours. The liquid now produced is known as wort.

Wort can be produced from the same grist a number of times, using higher temperatures each time. This process is known as sparging. In the seventeenth and eighteenth centuries the liquid produced at the third stage of the sparging was fermented, and produced small beer. What is finally left in the mash-tun at the end of the sparging, a substance known as spent-grains, is sold as animal food.

A slightly different method, known as decoction, is used for brewing lager beer. The grist and the liquor are combined at 80°F to 90°F, and then the temperature is raised to 150°F in the mash-tun.

Having obtained the wort, either by infusion or decoction, female hops are added and the liquid that now appears has a distinctly malty aroma, and is run into coppers, where it is boiled for two hours at about 215°F. The coppers usually hold thirty-six gallons.

The wort is then drawn off, quickly chilled to 60°F and conveyed to the fermenting vats or squares. These vats are about four or five feet deep. Yeast is now added, so that fermentation can take place. Yeast, which used to be called 'Godes good', is a form of living organism that works on the wort, and changes its chemical composition.

There are two forms of fermentation : top fermentation where the yeast rises to the surface of the wort, and bottom fermentation, where it sinks to the bottom. In most forms of ordinary beer, top fermentation is used, except with lagers, however, which are produced by bottom fermentation.

Beer has now been produced. Sometimes, if the result is not quite the right colour (customers can be extremely critical if their beer is off-colour) various caramels are used to bring it to the right shade.

After fermentation, the beer is allowed to rest in settling tanks for a few days. Other substances are sometimes added to give the beer a special finish. These are known as finings. The most common fining is Isinglass, which, incredibly, comes from the swimming bladder of a sturgeon. Sometimes, a few handfuls of dried hops are added to improve the taste.

Draught mild beers are then filtered and piped into barrels, where they are allowed to rest for a few days before being sent off to their customers. Lager beer is left to mature for one to nine months. In fact, it is called lager because that is the German word for storing. Where beers are bottled, they are often pasteurized, so that they can be stored for months, or years, as required.

1 Dr Samuel Johnson, who became involved briefly in managing Thrale's Brewery. This portrait by Sir Joshua Reynolds hangs in the head office of John Courage Ltd.

2 'Gin Lane'. Engraving after William Hogarth.

Chapter Five

Though beer may have replaced ale as the national drink by the end of the seventeenth century, the alehouse continued to be the place where beer was drunk. Sometimes the draw of the alehouse was too strong. When the East India Company was setting up its first expedition to the East in 1600, they provided their workmen with free beer on the site, in order to stop them going to the alehouse and thus delaying the work. When the three ships finally sailed, they took with them 150 barrels of beer to keep the crews happy during the long and hazardous voyage.

In the sixteenth and seventeenth centuries the alehouses were usually run by women. The ale-wife, as she was called, was a popular figure. Elynour Rummynge of Leatherhead operated during the reign of Henry VIII and though hideous, was so famous for the fine beers she served that people would come for miles just to sample them. Skelton wrote a long poem in praise of her, and she was considered at the time to be the Queen of the Ale-wives. Another famous ale-wife was Mother Louse of Hedington Hill. She was reputed to have been in 1673 the last woman in England to have worn a ruff.

One of the roles of beer about this time was that of consoling those in distress or trouble. Hugh Latimer had a goblet of spiced ale with his supper the night before he was burned alive, while Mary Queen of Scots, who was partial to the brown beer of Burton-on-Trent, had supplies of this excellent brew sent to her during her long captivity at Fotheringay. It helped her to pass the days until her execution in 1587. Sir Walter Raleigh, on the morning of his execution in 1618, treated himself to a cool tankard and a soothing pipe of tobacco.

For centuries, Church and State attempted to control or exploit the brewers. When the court moved about the countryside, as it often did, the king's servants seized, without payment, whatever they wanted, even down to such minor items as cheese and eggs. They had no compunction at all in raiding alehouses on the way and carrying off whatever might be needed.

Taxes of various kinds were imposed, fines for offences often of a trifling kind were levied. The brewers, as they became more numerous, retaliated by forming themselves into a protective society.

Most of the trades had created companies, or guilds, towards the end of the Middle Ages. These included famous companies such as the Mercers', Grocers' and Merchant Adventurers'. The company was the equivalent of a modern employers' association and a trade union combined.

On the one hand, these City Companies as they came to be known held a monopoly in a specific trade. Thus the Mercers' had the ribbon and silk monopoly. Queen Elizabeth I helped to make their fortune by being the first woman in England to wear silk stockings. As every other fashionable woman immediately followed her example there was a huge increase in the silk trade. In their gratitude to the enterprising Queen, the Mercers' Company made her a member of the company, the only woman ever to be so honoured.

At the same time, these City Companies protected their employees. Once a young man had been sworn in, the company made sure that he was paid the agreed minimum rates, that his conditions of work were healthy, that he was not being exploited by unscrupulous employers, and that his own chances of progress were recognized.

The system of combining in one body the representatives of both employers and employees worked extremely well in the unchanging and carefully controlled economy of the time. With only one large commercial centre, London, in existence, almost all trade passed through the city. It was therefore relatively simple for the guilds to keep a strong hold on the way a particular trade was developed.

The brewers in the City of London were originally grouped with innkeepers, cooks, piebakers and hucksters (street-sellers distributing goods without permit, or peddlars, beggars and the like); but by the reign of Henry IV (1399-1413) the brewers, although they had no royal charter as yet, formed their own 'Mystery', as a specific group of tradesmen or craftsmen were called.

They were known as the 'Free Brewers within the City'. They could elect a Master, two Wardens and five other members from both east and west of the Walbrook. These eight men were allowed to make regulations concerning the 'mystery' of brewing. They could arrange sales and hire employees. They had their own headquarters. They were specifically instructed to see that only good brews were made available, that the legal price was charged and that those who disobeyed these instructions were reported to the Chamberlain of the Court.

It must be recorded that the 'Free Brewers within the City' did not always adhere to these specifications. They seem to have been particularly dilatory at the time Richard Whittington was alive. This may have been partly due to the fact that Whittington was a mercer. He had come up, as legend has it, from Gloucestershire to London to make his fortune. It is more than likely that he had a cat. As the youngest son of a not very wealthy country squire, he would have had no personal income. Cats, on the other hand, were in tremendous demand for the city was overrun by mice and rats. Cats were scarce and a cat-owner could hire the animal out to a warehouse at a considerable price. No doubt Whittington's father was aware of this when he sent his twelve-year-old son off to London with his cat.

Whittington was apprenticed to a mercer and went into the ribbon trade, married his boss's daughter, and eventually became Master of the Mercers' Company and Lord Mayor of London.

There was often a good deal of rivalry between the City Companies, and the Free Brewers were probably not considered quite up to the expected standard. What is certain is that Sir Richard Whittington, whose term of office as Lord Mayor had come to an end, lodged a complaint that the Free Brewers were charging too much. The Master and twelve other 'worthy' members were ordered to appear at Guildhall on Thursday, 30 July, 1422.

Whittington's charge was that the Free Brewers had cornered the market in malt, by going out into the country and buying up all the barley in advance. They were thus able to push up the price when it came to selling to individual brewers.

The Company officials indignantly denied this, but the case

went against them and they were ordered to pay a fine of £20. This they refused to do. So they were ordered to be kept under lock and key in the Chamberlain's office until either they paid up or could find bail.

The Mayor and Aldermen then went off to lunch, leaving the Chamberlain very much embarrassed by his unwanted 'prisoners'. Eventually, finding no other solution and wishing to have lunch himself, he sent them home, telling them that the whole business had been done just to please Richard Whittington.

From records made at the time, it would seem that Whittington's annoyance arose originally from the fact that the Free Brewers had eaten 'fat swans at their feast on the morrow of St Martin'. This probably took place at their recently opened 'Brewershalle'. Perhaps they had omitted to invite the famous ex-mayor to this succulent meal.

Whittington had always taken an interest in the brewing trade. Earlier, he had granted the coopers, the men who made the barrels, their own distinctive trade-mark. This was duly recorded in the City Records and thenceforth had to be branded on every barrel.

Though the brewers continued to be harried by the city authorities they had a respite two years later when the mild-mannered John Michelle became mayor. The brewers prudently made sure of his goodwill by presenting him with a valuable ox that cost as much as twenty-one shillings and tuppence (£1.06p), and a boar that was even more expensive, at thirty shillings and a penny (£1.50½p). The new Mayor brought no trouble to the brewers, but contented himself with giving them the excellent advice that if they made good ale, he would have no reason to harry them.

The brewers complied.

It was not, however, until the sixteenth year of the reign of Henry VI, in 1438, that a Charter was formally granted to the Brewers' Company. This meant that the Mystery of Brewers of the City of London was now a corporate body. It was allowed to own land; and it was given the complete monopoly of brewing throughout the country for ever.

One of its first acts was to apply for a coat of arms. A few years later one was granted by William Hawkeslowe, Clarencieux King of Arms of the South Marches of Ingelond. The brewers' patron saints were St Mary and St Thomas the Martyr, otherwise Thomas à Becket, that troublesome archbishop who was murdered in Canterbury Cathedral in 1170. The official description of the arms, written in the usual complex terms of heraldry, runs : 'They beren asure thre barly sheues gold, bound of the same, a cheveron, gowles, in the cheveron thre barels, Sylvir, garnished with Sable.'

This in fact describes only the right half of the shield, which is blue with three gold sheaves of barley and three silver barrels set inside a chevron, or inverted triangular band. The other half of the shield contained the emblem of the martyred archbishop, daggers superimposed on a bishop's vestments in one panel, and three rather bleak-looking birds in another.

The whole effect was one of sensible and pleasing simplicity, a combination of practical and spiritual symbols. Even the most un-educated could understand the significance of the barley, the beer barrels and the daggers.

These arms, however, were not to last long. About a hundred years later Henry VIII decreed that Thomas à Becket was not a saint after all. The Brewers' Company was ordered to change their coat of arms, and promptly did so.

All reference to the unfortunate archbishop disappeared. The barrels and sheaves of barley remain, but they are surrounded by embellishments that distract the attention. A helmet has been added and above the whole elaborate design emerges a lady 'a demi Morien in her proper couler', as the complicated heraldic citation proclaims, holding in each hand three barley ears.

The Ancient Arms.

For the specialist (or the lover of crossword puzzles), the whole citation reads : 'Geules on a cheveron engrailed silver thre kilder-kyns sable hoped golde between syx barly sheues in saulte of the same, upon the Helme on a torse siluer and asur a demi Morien in her proper couler, vested asur, fretid siluer, the here golde, holding in either hande thre barly eres of the same manteled sable, dobled siluer.'

The brewers also built for themselves what Stowe described as a 'faire house' which, along with most of the City of London, was destroyed in the Great Fire of 1660.

Despite the granting of arms and other forms of official recognition, the brewers were still harassed from time to time. The wardens and the clerk were liable to be thrown into prison for non-compliance with the regulations or fined for the suspected brewing of inferior beer or for charging too high a price.

Elizabeth I's officials seem to have been particularly tiresome. Sometimes the production of beer was permitted, sometimes prohibited. The government fixed the price and even if this price was so low that the brewer lost money, he still had to go on brewing, otherwise he would be arrested as a rebel.

Perhaps Elizabeth's intransigent attitude sprang from the fact that the brewers had taken to burning coal, 'seacole' to be exact, instead of wood. A number of breweries were grouped around the Palace of Westminster where the Queen lived. The smoke from these breweries annoyed her enormously. So much so that in 1579 the short-tempered Queen, who had instructed the Lord Mayor to forbid brewers burning seacole while she was in residence at Westminster, had one brewer, John Platt, committed to prison for disobeying these orders. Thereafter the Brewers' Company under-took not to burn seacole in the breweries situated near her palace.

After Elizabeth, however, the authorities became less and less concerned with the rigid application of rules. Though the price of beer continued to be fixed by law, its strict application was no longer enforced.

The brewers were meanwhile becoming more powerful. The one-man businesses were giving place to family businesses, and to larger and larger concerns. As the individual brewers increased in wealth and strength, so the monopoly power of the Brewers' Company decreased.

By 1626, the Brewers' Company was complaining that they represented only six beer brewers and a few ale brewers out of the many hundreds of breweries now established throughout the country. So many breweries were now outside their control that they made no effort to try to recapture those outside London, or even those on the outskirts. They were content to ask the City Fathers to pass a decree that no one, within the limits of the city itself, should be allowed to set up a brewery unless they were Freemen of the City, and therefore a member of the Brewers' Company.

With the lifting of government restrictions and the decline of the monopoly power of the Brewers' Company, the brewers themselves began at last to improve both their financial prospects and their social standing. They were no longer equated with hustlers and began to invest their profits in land, to own estates and to aspire to the status of gentlemen.

The story of the wealthy brewer who had a coachman far too addicted to drink illustrates clearly how far the lowly brewer had advanced by the end of the seventeenth century.

This particular brewer, though fond enough of William his coachman, nevertheless eventually found it necessary to replace him by an abstainer. The brewer went on to say that if William had only kept off drink, he would have retained his place. William's reaction was immediate and memorable:

'Drink water,' cried William; 'had all men done so,
You'd never have wanted a coachman, I trow.
They are soakers, like me, whom you load with reproaches,
That enable you brewers to ride in your coaches.'

Chapter Six

The eighteenth century witnessed the great struggle between gin and beer.

At first sight, it might seem odd that these two drinks should be in opposition to each other. But, in fact, gin was also a native product and, like beer, it was made from grain. The main difference was that gin was distilled. An elaborate process of evaporation and condensation produced a far stronger drink than the more homely process of brewing.

But though so much stronger than beer, gin was cheaper. Brewers became distillers of the wonderful new drink. In London alone, one house in four became a gin shop. It could even be bought in the streets off wheelbarrows. One could get drunk for an outlay of one penny.

Not unnaturally, large numbers of the populace took to drinking gin as if it were water. The government, fearing a total moral collapse of the country, imposed a tax of twenty shillings on every gallon in 1736, and obliged retailers to pay £50 for a licence to sell gin.

Riots broke out immediately. Double guards were mounted at St James's Palace and other buildings. A detachment of guards was sent to Covent Garden to dissuade possible militants. On the day the Act came into force, 29 September, 1736, the signs of all the liquor shops were draped as a sign of mourning.

Naturally, the public soon found a way round the new Act. New 'chemist' shops appeared selling 'Cholick Water' that tasted remarkably like gin, and had exactly the same effect. In taverns gin was coloured and sold as wine, or given new names. 'Ladies' Delight' proved enormously popular.

The riots continued and the Act was modified, but despite fines and government intervention, the consumption of gin went up and up. The results were calamitous. A poet of the day wrote :

> Gin ! Cursed fiend with fury fraught,
>   Makes human race a prey,
> It enters by a deadly draught,
>   And steals our life away.

Hogarth, in his famous picture 'Gin Lane', depicts vividly the results of too much gin-drinking. In the foreground sits an early example of 'Mother's Ruin', a doped woman whose baby is falling from her arms. Behind are various signs of decrepitude, buildings falling down, murder and riot. Only the pawnbroker to the left is prospering, as gin-crazed citizens bring their pots to his well-built house.

Beer, on the other hand, was depicted as the saviour of mankind. The same poet who had such harsh words for gin had this to say of beer :

> Beer ! Happy produce of our isle,
>   Can sinewy strength impart,
> And, wearied with fatigue and toil,
>   Can cheer each manly heart.

Hogarth, too, produced a companion picture to 'Gin Lane' called 'Beer Street'. Here is a very different atmosphere. The city buildings are strong and well-kept. New construction work is under way. The plump, satisfied and healthy populace sit outside an inn, its prosperous-looking sign is being repainted. Tankards are much in evidence. The only man to suffer is the pawnbroker. His house is in ruins, his sign askew. He himself has barricaded himself in; and – an ironic touch – will only open a small hatch to take in a tankard himself.

This eighteenth-century struggle between beer and gin resulted in a firm belief that beer was wholesome, not only physically but mentally, while there was something morally wrong with gin. 'Gin palaces' became synonomous with an evil way of life; 'gin slinging' was a term of disapproval.

In the century that followed, the beneficial aspect of beer continued to be stressed, particularly by the Victorians. Indeed,

Victorian sociologists claimed that beer was the only consolation of the labouring classes. The manual labourer's prospects were considered dim. He worked from morning to night. There was nothing for him at the end of his life but the degrading prospect of the workhouse. His only consolation was his pint of wholesome beer at his supper. It fed him and cheered him up.

John Bickerdyke, in his fascinating book *The Curiosities of Ale and Beer* published in 1886, draws this very typical picture of the Victorians' attitude to the workman in his description of a labourer who had just finished his supper and his beer: 'Contentedly he smokes his pipes, chats sociably with his wife, and forgets for a while the many long days of hard work in store for him. Soon the soporific influence of the hop begins to take effect, and the toiler retires to rest, to sleep soundly, forgetful of the cares of life.'

Beer has thus become a panacea and a consolation, almost it would seem a means of keeping the labourer contentedly at work. Shut up the alehouses, Sundays or weekdays, and the poorer classes would take to the dram drinking. This insistence on the benefits of beer was not entirely due to a sociological need to keep labourers quiet and in their place. It was also a weapon in the strong prohibitionist movements that were a favourite of Victorian reformers.

Alcoholism was indeed extremely prevalent, and the prohibitionists had a point. There was a strong connection between drink and crime. The defenders would concede that spirits were dangerous, and would be the last to advocate a return to 'Gin Lane' days. But beer was a different matter. As long as it was pure, cheap and easy to obtain, it could do nothing but good.

Unlike in America in the 1930s (and India today) where prohibition became law, the abolitionists were never able, in the British Isles, to become more than a moral force. The Nonconformists, through religion, had more effect than the abolitionists. Whole sections of the population to this day believe that God disapproves of alcohol.

The abolitionists had to content themselves with thundering their warnings at a not too attentive audience, issuing tracts depicting the horrors of excessive drinking and forcing their audiences, by persuasion and sometimes threats, to 'take the pledge'. When they did so they swore, often on the Bible, never to touch alcohol as long as they lived. Finely decorated scrolls were awarded, to be

mounted and framed and hung proudly between mezzotint photo-
graphs of Mum and Dad on their wedding day.

But to the great majority of the people, the pint of bitter at the
end of a day's work was a natural part of life. For almost eighteen
centuries, first ale and then beer had sustained and cheered the
British. It would take more than a few 'cranks' as they were called,
to change all that.

The all-time record for beer drinking is believed to be held by
an eighteenth-century enthusiast called Jedediah Buxton, who, for
reasons one cannot fathom, kept a record of all the *free* drinks he
had accepted since the age of twelve. This amounted to the respectable total of 5,116 pints. It is not recorded how old he was when he
made this interesting calculation, but a man has to have downed
a very large number of winds, as he called pints because it only
took him one wind or breath to drink a pint (two winds for a quart),
before mine host starts pouring out the free drinks.

Labourers, however, were not the only people to be fond of beer,
or encouraged to drink it. A doctor, writing at the beginning of the
nineteenth century, tells how he escorted an attractive young lady
on an 'Opera Saturday' at the Crystal Palace; when he cautiously
suggested chocolate, lemonade or a vanilla ice as a refreshment, he
received the determined reply : 'Nonsense, Sir! Get me a pint of
stout immediately.'

University professors too have always traditionally been keen
followers of ale and beer. Brasenose College, Oxford, was long
famous for the strength of its own home-brewed ale. Specially
strong 'audit' ale is still brewed for Oxford colleges by Flowers, and
drunk by dons on certain days.

By the beginning of the nineteenth century, the large brewing
family, that now familiar institution, had begun to emerge. For
centuries the brewer had been one the humbler members of the
society. It was not until the end of the seventeenth century that
brewers, like the one who employed William the coachman, began
to make an impact. But they remained exceptions.

Jan Steen of Delph, who lived at the time of Charles II, is a good
example. His real ambition was to be a painter and eventually he
did become one. While he was still a brewer, however, he let the
brewery fall into disrepair. His wife, trying to encourage him to
brew again, said : 'You should bring life into the brewery'. Jan

Steen immediately went to the market and bought some live ducks.
Then he heated up some water, poured it with a little bit of malt
into a large pan, and set the ducks to swim on the warm mixture.
The ducks, not unnaturally, found the warm water hardly to their
liking, whereupon they leapt up into the air and flew about the
brewery quacking indignantly.

'My love,' said Jan Steen, turning to his wife, 'is it not lively now
in our brewery?'

William Hicks, the early eighteenth-century brewer to the royal
household, placed a statue of George I on top of the steeple of
Bloomsbury Church as a sign of his devotion to the King. Hum-
phrey Parsons, who as well as being a brewer was twice Lord
Mayor of London, hunted with Louis XV and, by giving the King
his horse as a present, was granted the privilege of supplying beer,
known as black champagne, to the French. To the King he was
always known as Le Chevalier de Malte Parsons.

However, these men were known for their eccentricities rather
than their power. It is in the eighteenth century that the great beer
families emerge: Whitbread, Worthington, Guinness, Allsopp,
Truman, Barclay, Perkins, Bass, Ind, Coope, and somewhat later,
Watney. These families, and others like them, began to expand
and take over the beer trade. They did this not by merger but by
marriage. Many of them had large families; mixing business and
marriage was a simple and satisfactory method of expanding.
These great beer families soon became known in the City as 'the
Princes of Trade'.

Their chief method of selling beer was through the 'tied house'
principle. Originally each hamlet had its own alehouse, run usually
by the brewer and his family, but as the brewers grew stronger the
habit began of supplying inns with the beers they needed. Many of
the innkeepers were not good businessmen, and went bankrupt.
The brewery would then buy up the business and it would become
a 'tied' inn. The advantage to the brewer was that he had a sure
outlet for his beer. He could also prevent his rivals from selling
their beer in the same place. The advantage to the customers was
that the brewer was financially strong enough to see that there was
always a sufficient quantity of beer.

There were, however, disadvantages. As the brewers had a monopoly in the supply of beer in a certain area, the question of variety

or even quality did not arise. The benefits of competition could be lost. Although most brewers took a pride in producing the best possible beer, some were not so meticulous and, particularly in the poorer districts, would use the tied inns to get rid of their inferior brews.

At the same time, the brewers let many of their inns and public houses to tenants; the only stipulation being that the tenant had to buy all his beer from the particular brewery. Here again there were advantages and disadvantages. An alert, enterprising and hard-working tenant could, by his own efforts, improve his inn and boost both his own profits and those of the brewer. His customers would benefit by improved conditions. On the other hand, a bad tenant could let the business fall away, and there was nothing either the brewer or the customers could do. There were cases where the tenant would allow only his personal friends into a public house, and serve only those he liked.

These great brewing families were very different from the humble suppliers of ale to the medieval hamlet. Many of them were the friends of kings and some sought titles. Henry Allsopp became Lord Hindlip of Hindlip, while Michael Bass's son, also of Burton-on-Trent, became Lord Burton of Rangemore. The Guinness family, providers of the black Dublin 'Liffey Water', also took titles. Benjamin Truman was knighted by George III. Many, like Samuel Whitbread, the son of the founder of Whitbread's, went into Parliament. He was known as 'Mr Whitbread the Politician' and like most of the other parliamentary brewers, was a strong supporter of the Liberal Party.

Not all brewers were so successful. One of the least satisfactory and most surprising brewers was the great Doctor Samuel Johnson himself. It would seem that, when not engaged with his dictionary or keeping Boswell and his coffee-house friends supplied with anecdotes, he was busy with the brewery owned by Mr Thrale.

It is true that he was not fully involved until Mr Thrale's death, when he, Mrs Thrale and three men, Cator, Smith and Crutchley, were made executors. With his usual self-assurance he immediately appointed himself chairman; but he was not a born brewer and although in some years the profit rose to £15,000, in others it tottered, as Mrs Thrale wrote, 'twice upon the verge of bankruptcy.'

It was decided in the end to sell the business. Once again, Dr Johnson could not resist taking the leading role. He could be seen dashing about with his ink-horn and pen supervising this and that, with an apposite phrase ever on his lips. He would startle sober-headed and cautious enquirers with the words : 'We are not here to sell a parcel of boilers and vats, but the potentiality of growing rich beyond the dreams of avarice.'

In the end the brewery was sold to Robert Barclay and John Perkins for £135,000.

Chapter Seven

The history of beer in the twentieth century is very much a story of new legislative restraints and regulations. The violent expansion of the Victorian era had brought hardships as well as benefits. Liberal consciences fought for reforms in all spheres of life. Beer was not exempt.

In 1901 the Intoxicating Liquor (Sale to Children) Act, known also as the Child Messenger Act, forbade the sale of most alcoholic drinks to children under fourteen. Although this had undoubtedly a good effect, one cannot help feeling that Jedediah Buxton would have disapproved. His record of free drinks would have been considerably reduced had he been obliged to wait until he was fourteen before starting on his life's work.

The Act also stipulated that the justices' annual licensing meeting was to be held in the first fortnight of February and no structural alterations were to be made to public houses without their approval. Only army and navy canteens were excused from having a licence. Other sections of the Act gave the police power, for the first time, to arrest drunkards in public places or in charge of children under seven. Protection for the wives of habitual drunkards was also introduced.

Private drinking clubs were, for the first time, required to register, and could be closed down if the magistrates thought fit.

These first attempts at regulating the country's drinking habits were followed, in 1915, by much more radical and extensive ones.

The outbreak of war in 1914 revealed that there was a large part of the population, particularly among the poorer section, who were physically deficient from excessive drinking. The authorities were horrified at the number of recruits who had to be turned away for failing to reach the required standard of fitness.

It was as much to improve the physique of the newly-created civilian armies as to provide better conditions that the Defence of the Realm Act, better known as D.O.R.A., and its various amendments were introduced in 1914 and 1915.

It was stressed that D.O.R.A. was a temporary war-time Act that would be repealed as soon as peace returned.

Its most important effect was the creation of the Central Control Board which could, without reference to higher authority, vary the licensing hours, buy up breweries, inspect premises, forbid drinks like absinthe from being sold and even sell drink itself. The state-owned pubs of Carlisle are a survival from the days of the Board's control.

The only way the authorities could think of cutting down alcoholism was to curtail the hours when drink could be served. The fact that the moderate drinker in search of a convivial outing or the traveller thirsty after a long haul suffered as a result was considered unimportant, compared to the gain in 'cannon fodder' the country would obviously obtain.

The establishment of set hours when drink could be served was a complete innovation – and not a very welcome one. Pub opening hours became a feature of daily life. 'Time, gentlemen please' at the same hour each evening became a recognized signal for the hurried pouring down a throat of that extra pint or two. The notices about fines for drinking after hours, the bustling efforts to get rid of customers, indeed the whole way of life built around opening hours, were all due to D.O.R.A.'s interference.

Luckily, everybody said, it will end when the war does.

But regulations have a nasty habit of surviving. No doubt the civil servants with responsibility for administration of the new law were keen to keep it going. If it was abolished, they might lose their jobs. And then again, the health of the average man did improve. Alcoholism was reduced.

So D.O.R.A. stayed.

There were abortive efforts to shift her. But the tendency at first was to increase or merely alter marginally the existing law. In 1923 it became illegal to sell drink to anyone under eighteen. The only exception was the sale of beer and cider to somebody over sixteen as long as it was to be drunk with a meal.

In 1934 there was a slight relaxation, mainly for the benefit of farm workers, when at certain times of the year, at the discretion of the magistrates, drinking hours could be extended from 10 p.m. to 10.30 p.m.

The 1939-45 War saw the zoning of beer introduced to cut down transport problems. All public houses within a certain area had to be supplied by the same brewery. This meant that in many parts of the country there was little or no choice of brew, for although the large breweries were to a certain extent exempt from this regulation, there was little they could do in supplying other districts.

Beer became standardized to, many claimed at the time, a very low standard. It was rationed too, like practically everything else, and the brewers operated a system whereby if one was hit by bombs the others came to its help.

Many public houses were destroyed and others were allowed to fall into disrepair through a shortage of building materials and the difficulties of getting building permits. In 1945 the Licensing Planning Act was introduced to control the redevelopment of public houses in bombed areas.

There were still agitators for the repeal of the original D.O.R.A., but the Licensing Act of 1953 merely consolidated the previous Acts, including a new measure allowing passenger aircraft to obtain a licence without having to go through a justices' court.

The Hotel Proprietors Act of 1956 distinguished between hotels and inns; while the Licensing Act of 1961 introduced the restaurant licence, the residential licence and the combined restaurant and residential licence.

There was at the same time a slight easing of D.O.R.A.'s hold. Opening and closing hours could be changed from one part of the country to another. Then ten minutes 'drinking-up time' allowed, when no further drinks could be served, that the beer already in one's glass could be drunk.

At the same time, Wales, which for religious reasons had been 'dry' on Sundays for many years, was allowed to decide, region by region, whether to allow Sunday drinking. Many did so.

Today, with Britain's return after a century and half to her traditional European role and her entry into the European Economic Community, further changes will undoubtedly be seen.

The challenge from French, German and Danish beers in particular has already led many brewers to experiment with new brews. The need to cater for Continental taste, which tends towards lager, is forcing breweries to adopt a more outward-looking approach.

But oddly enough it is in, literally, the field of hops that the greatest change will be seen. The hops used in Europe are the fat, juicy, female type. The male, a thin, stringy but persistent fellow has always been rigorously barred from Continental hop fields. But not in Britain.

Secure upon an island, more tolerant, or perhaps merely ignorant of the hop's love-life, British hop-farmers have allowed the weedy male, though of no practical use, to live in the ditches close to the beloved females.

Though so small, he is reputed to be an ardent, passionate and above all, extremely rapid performer, and can cover more ground in a night than many slower plants achieve in a season.

The bosomy female hops of Kent had nothing to complain about.

But now, alas, all is to be different.

Continental brewers, particularly those engaged in producing lager, insist that the taste of a fertilized hop is different. The 'married' lady-hop is sweeter than she was in her virginal state. British hop-growers may disagree, but recognize that if they wish to sell on the European market they will have to produce unfertilized hops. This has led to a ruthless campaign of extermination. The hoes are out in the British hop fields, digging out the male wherever he may be hiding.

But though so small and insignificant, he is a tenacious fellow, and can lie hidden at the bottom of a ditch for months, only to spring suddenly into existence, and with his amazing virility, destroy in a night the farmer's careful plans.

The battle goes on.

With Britain in Europe, it would seem again as if the end of D.O.R.A. must now surely be in sight. European countries have never had licensing hours. Cafés, bistros, beer-kellers and ristorientes open and close when they like. It has always been possible, after a long mountain trek for instance, to stop at half-past three at a foreign inn and have a cooling draught of lager.

Continental habits are expected to be adopted increasingly in the British Isles, along with decimalization, metrication and the other systems in use in Europe. Surely tough old D.O.R.A. will not be able to hold out much longer? Or will she, in order to survive, adopt the nationalist mantle and declare that, despite the evidence of history, it is somehow British to have strictly regulated opening and closing hours? We shall see.

In the meantime the brewing trade 'progresses'. Mergers are the pattern of the day. Machines work out the advantages and costs of a take-over bid, and operators, who have never been in the brewing business at all, suddenly find themselves controlling great chains of breweries throughout the country. After all, they claim, beer is a commodity like any other. It's executives, not individuals, you need today. It does not matter whether a family or a computer controls the organization of a business. It is the end product that counts.

Yet because of beer's social significance and its closeness to people's daily life, it seems unlikely that, however large and remote the controlling bodies may grow, the brewery trade will become utterly bureaucratic. The Saxons' almost religious devotion to ale lives on, as a visit to a public house on a Saturday evening will quickly demonstrate.

The British are still the dedicated drinkers they have always been.

Part Two

Social Graces

Chapter Eight

The alehouse, or its equivalent, has always had a special place in the social life of the British Isles.

The Romans were the first to build *tabernae* (or *tavernae*) at regular intervals along the straight, military roads that spread across the country. Here, in these earliest roadside inns, food and a bed for the night could be found. The *tabernae* were not, strictly speaking, places of entertainment or relaxation, but practical staging posts.

But in addition to these somewhat severe lodging-houses, not unlike the modern youth hostels, there sprang up, particularly during the period of Roman-Britannic civilization, more sophisticated inns and public houses built in the Roman style. These would usually be two-storey buildings, with a dining room on the upper floor. A common drinking vessel was provided, and sometimes flagons chained to posts. On the hard tables and benches games would be played, chess being a favourite. In some inns the door or even the whole front of the building would be decorated like a chessboard to remind travellers that the game could be played there. To this day *Chequers* is a common name for an inn.

With the departure of the Romans and the arrival of the Saxons, the international character of the country disappeared. No longer was Rome the central point. Small, self-governing, parochial areas replaced the large, empire-conscious tracts of land. Roman inspectors no longer travelled all the way from Italy to Scotland, fastidiously making inventories of even the smallest details of daily life.

The *tabernae* fell into disuse through lack of customers and because, in their exposed positions along the now undefended roads, they were liable to attack from bands of robbers. The peacefulness imposed and maintained by Roman rule, an order that had

55

become accepted over the centuries as normal, was now replaced
by insecurity and violence. For the first time for over three hundred
years private citizens banded together to form well-armed groups.
Villages and hamlets surrounded themselves with walls and forti-
fications.

Though many sighed for the peaceful era of the Roman Occupation and tried vainly to recapture it, the remainder did the best
they could.

The *tabernae* were replaced by alehouses. These were altogether
more modest institutions, housed in a cottage that was no different
from any other in the hamlet. No accommodation was provided.
Travellers had to depend on the hospitality of monks or, later on,
great landowners who would often set aside a special house or part
of a building for this purpose.

The arms of the lord of the manor would be displayed at such
buildings so that they could be recognized, but the humbler alehouses were content with sticking a pole over the front door and
tying a branch of a tree or bush on to it, as a sign of their function.

For a long time the alehouse and the monastic or seigneural
lodging-house were the only form of inn in the country. While the
'locals' gathered at 'The Bush', travellers would call in at the large
halls of the monasteries and manors. Tales and news from afar
would be exchanged at the latter, gossip at the former.

Names and addresses of guests would be recorded by the bureaucratic monks, a practice that is still carried out by hotel proprietors,
but at the alehouses, where everybody knew everybody, there was
no need to do so. The habit of never prying into another person's
business or even asking his name, but accepting him as he is, which
is so characteristic of a pub, is no doubt a result of the cosy famil-
iarity of the old alehouses.

There is no record of the number of alehouses in existence during
the Middle Ages; each hamlet probably had one. There were no
large cities. Monasteries and castles were relatively scarce and
widely scattered, and not all of them supplied food and lodging.
Travelling must have been a thirsty business unless one was
prudent enough to carry one's own supplies. Even in the sixteenth
century, when towns had begun to appear, there was a scarcity of
inns.

A regulation dated 1552 prescribed that there were not to be more than forty taverns in London. Other cities fared even worse : Bristol was allowed six; while Hull, Exeter, Gloucester, Chester, Canterbury and Newcastle-upon-Tyne had to make do with four. Salisbury, Hereford, Worcester, Southampton, Colchester and Winchester were allowed only three. Cambridge could have four, but Oxford three. No doubt the legislator was a Cambridge man. However, this state of affairs did not last long. Forty years later a report by the Queen's Council in 1591 informed the government that there were so many alehouses in Cheshire and Lancashire that on a Sunday no one went to church except the curate and his clerk.

By the following century the spread of alehouses and inns had accelerated. In 1639 there were twenty-four alehouses in Covent Garden alone. Seven years earlier Decker had reported that there were whole streets consisting of a continuous line of alehouses, with 'not a shop to be seen between red lattice and red lattice'. The lattice was placed across the open window of the alehouse to prevent wives and other inquisitive people from seeing who was drinking inside.

From being places where travellers could find rest and shelter or where locals could gossip, the inn became a recognized centre for social, artistic, literary and financial activity.

Shakespeare, Ben Jonson, Marlowe, Beaumont and Fletcher frequented the *Falcon Tavern* at Bankside. It was here that Fuller witnessed and described a 'wit combat' between Ben Jonson and Shakespeare. He compared Ben Jonson to a Spanish galleon; he was 'higher in learning; solid, but slow'. Shakespeare, on the other hand, was like an English man-of-war, 'lesser in bulk, but lighter in sailing'. He could turn with all tides, tack about and 'take advantage of all winds by the quickness of his wit and invention'.

The Elizabethans were great frequenters of inns and alehouses. Ben Jonson liked the *Swann* at Charing Cross, where the drawer's name was Ralph.

'God bless them all, and keep them safe,
And God bless me, and God bless Ralph,'

wrote Jonson when called upon, after Elizabeth's death, to say grace to the new monarch, James. James, it is recorded, was so pleased that he gave Ben Jonson a hundred pounds.

Other inns visited by Ben Jonson's gregarious group included the *Dog,* the *Sun,* the *Triple Tun,* and the *Devil* in Fleet Street. This inn was named in honour of St Dunstan who, when tempted by Satan, took the Devil by the nose :

> With red hot tongs he made him roar
> Till he was heard three miles or more.

It was run by an innkeeper called Sim Wadlow, 'the King of Skinkers' (a 'skinker' being a tapster; derived from the old English verb *schencken* : to pour out) as Jonson called him, a fine-looking man with a short beard and moustaches, a ruff and a rakish hat. It was at the *Devil* that Jonson and his friends held their Apollo Club meetings where the jests were said to be as lively as the drink.

Then there was the famous *Mermaid* in Bread Street. 'What things have we seen/ Done at the Mermaid ?' asked Beaumont in a piece of juvenile verse. Here Jonson and Shakespeare would fight it out again : the galleon of learning against the English man-of-war with 'little Latin and lesser Greek'. Shakespeare was an adept at punning. On being made godfather to one of Jonson's children, he said he would give a gift of 'a dozen good latten spoons [an inferior metal], and thou shalt translate them.'

Shakespeare seems to have had a number of godchildren, and some, if rumour was right, could have done without the prefix 'god'. One of these more closely related 'god'-children was reputed to be Sir William Davenant, whose 'real' father had been the landlord of the *Crown* at Oxford where the dramatist often stayed on his journeys between Stratford and London.

It was not Shakespeare, however, but the great Dr Johnson in the eighteenth century who was to give the concept of tavern life its finest accolade. In a magnificent outburst he pointed out that nobody could be truly at their ease in a private house. The master was too anxious to please, the guests too determined to be agreeable. Only in a tavern could one be sure of a complete welcome, utterly unrestricted by the cares of social etiquette. He concluded his peroration with the memorable words : 'No Sir; there is nothing which has yet been contrived by man, by which so much happiness is produced, as by a good tavern or inn.'

Samuel Johnson favoured a number of inns, all in or near Fleet

Street. The *Mitre,* situated in Mitre Court, was the scene of Boswell's first meeting with Johnson. Boswell records with pride how they went there at nine in the evening and had a good supper and port wine. He was so impressed that he wrote of that evening : 'The orthodox, High Church sound of the Mitre – the figure and manner of the celebrated Samuel Johnson – the extraordinary power and precision of his conversation, and the pride from finding myself admitted as his companion, produced a variety of sensations and a pleasing elevation of mind beyond what I had ever experienced.' Thus began that great literary association.

The *Devil Tavern,* so much loved by Ben Jonson, was also a favourite of Dr Johnson's. It was here that he sat down one evening to a dinner that did not end until daybreak. The inn was finally pulled down in 1788.

Opposite stood the *Cock Tavern* that had an effigy of a cock over the door, carved, it was reputed, by Grinling Gibbons. It was to the *Cock* that Pepys went one night and, he records, drank, ate a lobster, sang and was 'mighty merry'. Later he 'carried Mrs Pierce home'; and then returned with Knipp to the Temple in order to cross the river by boat to Foxhall to watch the bonfire lit in celebration of Charles II's coronation.

The river in those days was a common and cheap means of transport, particularly for those going on a 'pub crawl'. Yet the inns and taverns themselves, apart from two above Tower Bridge and one at Battersea, rarely faced the river. This was partly because seafaring men, home from a long journey, did not want to look at water, but mainly because there was no embankment and the river line varied with the tides and weather.

Another literary frequenter of Fleet Street taverns was Oliver Goldsmith. He would often appear at the *Mitre,* though the *Globe Tavern* was probably his favourite, because of a huge man who used to call in there and sing a popular song, celebrating the supposed fact that Bacchus, the God of Wine

> . . . sprang from a barrel of Nottingham Ale,
> Nottingham Ale, boys; Nottingham Ale; no liquor
> on earth is like Nottingham Ale.

Writers and poets, however, were not the only people to use the taverns as meeting places and even centres of inspiration. Business was often conducted in the tavern. Lloyds Insurance was said to have started in a tavern, and the sale of stocks and shares was originally conducted in the same way. The habit of accepting a man's word or bond across the board or bench derived from this practice. Solicitors' clerks and other 'learned' gentlemen would earn a few pennies drawing up legal documents, witnessing wills, conveyances or other matters. The legal gentlemen would always be found at the same spot in the same tavern. Business would be conducted amicably and to everyone's satisfaction over a mug of beer. This practice still flourishes in many parts of the country, and the bar-room lawyer has given his clients much legal assistance at a very modest price.

Politicians, too, were great frequenters of inns. They tended to form themselves into clubs. Thus, in Swift's day, the *Bell Tavern* in King Street, Westminster, was the meeting place of the October Club. This anti-Whig Club was so-named because of the great quantities of October Ale that its hundred or so members managed to pour down their throats every evening.

The most persistent political club, however, was the Everlasting Club. It started during the Civil War, and got its name from the fact that it never closed, but sat night and day, every day of the week, month and year. This mammoth task was performed by relays of drinkers who would take over one from the other. Its original political purpose was soon forgotten, but it is recorded that the members of the Everlasting Club, before they finally collapsed from sheer exhaustion, managed to smoke fifty tons of tobacco and put away thirty thousand butts of ale over a period of approximately fifty years.

Another type of political club was the Mug House. A number of such clubs were set up to celebrate the arrival of the Protestant House of Hanover, and the accession of King George I. They were intended to be centres of Protestant loyalty. The name derived from a line of mugs hanging outside the tavern. But the Mug House clubs became so violent, starting a 'loyal' riot at the least excuse, that they eventually had to be banned by an Act of Parliament. Mug House clubs, however, continued for many years as centres of social activity, each member having his own personal mug.

With the coming of the Victorians, and their strict middle-class

sense of respectability and rectitude, the inn or tavern lost much of its status. It was no longer considered the proper place for a gentleman of taste or learning to be found. The clubs of the Mall, and their provincial equivalents, replaced the taverns as meeting places for wits, writers, men of fashion, sportsmen and politicians.

The public house, as the tavern came to be called, catered for those who belonged to no club. Its emphasis was upon cosy seclusion. Each bar was rigorously separated from the next: there would be a public bar and a saloon bar, where drinks were slightly more expensive, thus immediately creating a social barrier. The working-class men would gather in the public bar while the lower middle-class clerk on his way home from the office looked in at the saloon bar. It would be almost as inconceivable for an habitué of the public bar to be seen in the saloon bar as vice versa. Each stayed strictly within his artificially created social sphere.

There were other bars too. The private bar was usually a small area partitioned off between the main bars where it would be possible to sit without being seen by anybody except the barman. Swivelling lattice windows would sometimes be built into the partitions so that discreet peeps at the other drinkers could be given. It was rather like being in a confessional. Also provided with lattice windows was the ladies bar. In those very pre-Lib days it was not considered at all proper for a lady to frequent a public house, where such notorious pastimes as billiards took place, even with a man; and certainly not on her own.

This taboo extended right through society. Indeed it was perhaps more rigidly applied by the working-class population than the middle-class. The upper classes, male or female, would never dream of being seen in a pub. This exclusion of women, except on festive occasions, may have had something to do with the male determination to get away from female company for a while. Just as the exclusive clubs were for men only, so the pub followed the same trend.

Only in the ladies bar could women gather secretly, chortle over their stout and cast, through their purdah-like windows, flirtatious glances at their lords and masters next door. Such behaviour, however, was not considered to be very ladylike.

The pubs, unlike the inns and taverns before them, were no longer meeting places for artists and writers. The large rooms above the actual bars would be let out to Working Men's Clubs, to musical and other societies, and to wedding parties.

These strictly enforced and accepted divisions were a reflection of the divisions within the general structure of Victorian society. In miniature, the pub contained all the taboos and class boundaries of that society.

Yet each division, though separate from its neighbour, contained within itself a tremendous conviviality and vigour. Once accepted, at whatever level, all personal barriers were down. A man could often find more genuine friendship and conviviality in his local bar than at his home. No one pried or enquired into his affairs, no one lectured or nagged him, no one expected more of him than he was prepared to give. In these warm, jovial surroundings a man could forget for a while the harshness of the outside world.

The Victorian-style public house survived until well after the Second World War; but with the breaking down of social barriers, the accelerating emancipation of women, the improvement in home standards and the increasing influence of America and the Continent on the British way of life, the intimate, secluded and convivial public house gave way to open, undivided bars where all, supposedly classless and equal, could drink their new brands in cheerful harmony.

Victorian-style public houses can still be found, particularly in the quieter and more conservative parts of the country. Some brewers have even gone to the extent of recreating these pubs. Foreign capitals will reproduce down to the last pewter mug and brass coach-horn the 'English' public house. But in its home country, that type is being rapidly replaced by the open-planned, one-bar establishment.

Perhaps these new-style inns with their greater freedom and wider appeal will once again attract every kind of customer. Perhaps a future Dr Johnson in a futuristic *Mitre* will hold court again among the wits and creative men of that happy day.

Chapter Nine

Historians of cricket are somewhat hesitant in discussing the origins of the game. One fact they agree on. Official, organized cricket matches began in the eighteenth century, and among the very earliest were those played on the cricket field at Hambledon, a little village in Hampshire. For it was here that Richard Nyren, landlord of the *Bat and Ball* inn, organized a series of matches that have since earned Hambledon the title of 'the cradle of English cricket'. Captaining a local team, Nyren challenged all comers.

So well did his team perform that his rivals sought players from all over England. Thus was formed the first 'all England' team. Even so, Richard Nyren defeated all challengers twenty-nine times. The rewards, besides the refreshing tankards of beer, were sometimes unusual. On one occasion, the losing side were required to provide 'eleven pairs of white corded dimity breeches and eleven handsome striped pink waistcoats' for the lucky winners to wear.

The *Bat and Ball* still stands today beside the village green where the great breeches and waist-coat game was played. Cricket is still played there.

A. G. Macdonell in his book *England, Their England* gave perhaps the best description of a village cricket match ever to be found in English literature. The match was based on a real one that took place at Fordcomb in Sussex in the 1930s. The visiting London team was gathered together by Sir John Squire, poet, editor and expert on public houses. (He himself claimed that he knew the name and history of every public house in the country.)

His team, consisting mainly of writers, editors, publishers and journalists, was formed largely through casual meetings over friendly drinks in bars. Squire, a keen cricketer himself, would enquire of any new acquaintance whether he was interested in

3 A modern hop picker.

4 An illustration from Reynolde Scot's *A Perfite Platform of a Hoppe Garden* (1574). The methods and tools used in hop picking have remained basically unchanged.

5 'The Crown of Hops' by W. F. Witherington, painted c. 1830. 6 Hop pickers at Staplehurst in Kent, 1972.

cricket. If the answer was yes, his name would be jotted down in a small notebook and an invitation to join a team on a Sunday afternoon would eventually arrive. The matches were played against village teams.

These weekly summer expeditions to the surrounding countryside continued up to the Second World War. They were discontinued throughout the war but as soon as peace returned again, Sir John Squire, or Jack Squire as he preferred to be called, decided to start up his weekly cricket visits again.

He was based in, or perhaps one should say, moored at, the *Markham Arms* in King's Road, Chelsea. The pub still had its old Victorian appearance; there was a public bar, a saloon bar, a private bar and a tiny ladies bar, with a line of hand-painted glass vents which could be spun round to reveal the identity of the ladies in that very exclusive and secluded place. It was then run by Mrs Andrews, 'Ma Andrews' as she was called. She was at first sight rather formidable. Her face, of a reddish hue, seemed to be permanently crumpled up. She would sit on her stool, watching her clientele through almost closed eyes. Her voice grated. Sometimes she would vanish for hours up to her flower-bedecked, bottle-strewn private room upstairs. She always wore tight, fitted suits that had had some difficulty in keeping her ample figure under control. Once a year she would appear in a magnificently feathered hat and boa and have herself driven off, in a hired car, to the annual Licensed Victuallers' Ball.

Jack Squire, a rotund, untidy, elderly comet would appear from time to time. He always produced a crumpled list of possible players from his pocket and, holding it up close to his eyes (for he was enormously short-sighted) would stare at it anxiously. As his hand usually shook violently it was a wonder he could ever decipher what was written on this list.

The difficulty was increased by the fact that the paper or papers often contained notes for forthcoming articles and the names of young writers he was encouraging (he was the best and most painstaking a mentor an author could have) so that the composition of a *Markham Arms* cricket team on any Sunday was a complete mystery to all concerned.

Some kind of cohesion, it is true, was brought to the business by his second-in-command, Patrick Howarth, who was to write *Play Up, and Play the Game,* an account of the public school-type hero. At this time, however, he was about to be demobilized as a major from Army Intelligence, and was seeking an entry into the Foreign Service.

By some kind of fluke, twelve to fifteen assorted people would eventually meet at the indicated railway station and set off for the country. The teams were rarely the same two Sundays running. It was always a struggle to get people to give up their weekly lie-in and there were numerous casualties from hang-overs.

A few 'distinguished' authors, friends of Jack Squire, would turn up in full-blazered glory, complete with caps and cricket bags. Some even brought their own bats. But the rest were a fairly mixed lot. There was Bertie Boret. He had been, it was true, a Cambridge Blue; but he had won it for rowing, not cricket. He had a stentorian voice which was useful for encouraging others, an enormous laugh, and an apparently endless capacity for downing pints. His customary position was in deep field. He once played at a match where there was a steep hill beyond him; the ball was always running down the hill. Bertie, fed up with the toil of chasing down and carrying up the ball, borrowed a bicycle and would disappear over the hill in pursuit of a mighty hit, shouting 'Tally-ho!'

Then there was Robin Green. He was an archaeologist and spent much of the week grovelling around the mud banks of the Thames at low tide looking for medieval coins. He was the *Markham Arms* team's official umpire. Somewhat absent minded, and unable to remember how many balls had been bowled, Green devised a system of transferring at each delivery, a medieval coin, groat or such like, from one pocket to another. Unfortunately he rarely had the exact number of coins ready so that sometimes an over would last two balls, sometimes ten.

His mind rarely deviated from historical matters. Once during a tea-break at a small country village, an indignant woman broke into the pavilion and said that one member of the visiting team was digging up all her vegetables, and would someone do something about it, as she couldn't make him see sense.

It was Robin Green. When Jack Squire and Pat Howarth told him that he shouldn't dig up the poor woman's vegetables, he retorted plaintively that he wasn't after the vegetables but the magnificent medieval dump he believed lay underneath them.

Mrs Andrews took an enormous pride in 'her' team, and the day before a match would slip Pat Howarth £20 or more to be used as he thought fit. This would usually be expended on beer in the country public houses that invariably served as rendezvous.

On one occasion, Jack Squire devised the brilliant strategy of getting to the inn in question as early as possible. He had, he said, already invited the opposing team to meet the *Markham Arms* heroes there. His idea was that the *Markham Arms* team would ply their opponents with drink, while drinking nothing themselves but lemonade, so that when play commenced at 3 p.m. the London team would have the distinct advantage of sobriety.

Mrs Andrews gave a larger than usual contribution. The team set off from Waterloo in a determined mood. They had never won a match, but this time it seemed as if the strategy could not fail.

The rendezvous inn was a pleasant old-fashioned place. The day was mild and dry. Dense, shady trees formed a shield round the cricket field outside the inn. Insects and birds did what was expected of them. Already that particular drowsiness that seems to typify village cricket lay over the pitch. It was, indeed, a perfect summer day.

All that was missing was the opposing team. After a decent interval, Bertie Boret suggested that an attempt should be made to slake their thirst. It was then discovered that the inn carried no lemonade; the publican believing firmly than anything non-alcoholic rotted the guts. So there was no option. The local beer proved excellent and Ma Andrews' cash soon began to vanish.

At five minutes to three the opposing team appeared, fresh, sober, and eager for the game. The London players, staggering a little, had some difficulty in getting onto the field at all.

The villagers won the toss. They batted first and made a record score of 285 for 3 declared (two of their players retired voluntarily to let others have a go, and one knocked himself out with his own bat when trying for a third six in succession).

The *Markham Arms* team made 19 all out. Most of these were byes.

However, their spirits were undaunted and their return to London almost as triumphant as if they had won. Mrs Andrews seemed perfectly satisfied with the result and went on contributing in the same liberal way, until she retired some years later, and the *Markham Arms* was taken over by a management who did not have the same interest in village cricket.

English sport has always been connected with inns and the imbibing of beer. Apart from the many inns overlooking country cricket fields, there is the famous tavern at Lords where much cricket had been discussed over appropriate tankards.

Although football started as a street game in overpopulated cities, an even older form of the game has been played for centuries between the villages of Hallaton and Medbourne in Leicestershire.

The day starts with a service in Hallaton church. After this, a huge hare pie is distributed by the rector on a piece of land known as Hare Pie Bank. The cost of producing the pie is met from a bequest made by a lady who was saved from being gored by a bull by the sudden appearance of a hare. The bull's attention was distracted long enough for the lady to escape. In a fit of gratitude to her animal saviour she decreed that his descendants should be eaten by hers on this very field every Easter-time.

After the feast the two sides, in unlimited numbers, take the field. The 'football' is a small keg of beer. It is thrown onto the ground and the game begins.

The object of the men from Medbourne is to get the keg over a boundary stream about three-quarters of a mile away; while those from Hallaton aim at another boundary stream in the other direction.

When the first keg has reached its goal, a second is put into play. When this has been scored, it is the turn of a third. The game can (for it is still played) go on for hours. When it is over, the teams drink the kegs they have scored.

It may not be quite as sophisticated as modern football but it has its advantages. No professional player has yet worked out how to drink, as well as score, his goals.

Games have always been popular in inns. The ancient game of bumble-puppy used to be played extensively. Now it is only to be found in the remoter inns of the countryside. It consists basically of a board with a number of wooden pegs or pins on it. In the centre stands a short pole. From the top of the pole is suspended a ball on the end of a length of string. Each player in turn swings the ball around the pole. As it revolves at the end of the string, it sweeps backwards and forwards across the board, knocking over any pins it may encounter. The winner is the one who knocks over the most pins.

The game of nine-pins was played mainly out of doors. The modern, sophisticated ten-pin bowling alley (the number of pins was changed from nine to ten for legal reasons) is a further extension of the original game; but now, as is so often the case, it is completely divorced from its original location : the inn.

Shove-halfpenny has long been a favourite game. The smooth board, polished by keen innkeepers with a rag dipped in ale, and smoother halfpennies are still a traditional part of a country inn's equipment. Dominoes, too, hold their fascination. In certain pubs in London and other cities, domino clubs are still popular. Office workers during their work-break will make for their favourite seat and play dominoes. Championships are organized. It is a serious game, needing skill and concentration, not to be interrupted by the vulgarity of canned music or other vociferous distractions.

Darts, now perhaps the most popular of all pub games, is a relatively new one, hardly a hundred years old. Darts reached their highest popularity during the Second World War when the pubs may have been short of beer but made up for it in dart-boards. Every barrack room and tent had one. The dart-board was even declared an official part of the necessary equipment of the British

army that crossed to Normandy in June 1944. Every landing-ship
and unit had amongst its store of guns, ammunition and rations, its
standard, therapeutic dart-board and complementary darts. The
boards were then made of wood – a pity, because the darts rarely
stuck into them.

Many of the United States troops stationed in southern England
waiting for D-Day discovered darts in English country pubs and
took the game with them, first to Normandy and then back home
to the States. A recent result of this was the installation in the
American Skylab, orbiting the world, of a dart-board, complete
with magnetic-headed darts to counteract the effect of weightless-
ness.

But darts were not only a recreation. There was a plan to turn
them into weapons of war.

There was in the 1940s at General Headquarters in London,
situated in the old St Paul's School building in Hammersmith, a
department known as the Bright Idea Department. Here was sent
any suggestion received from the general public on how to win or
better prosecute the war. Some of the ideas were bizarre to say the
least. One enthusiast suggested building a raft the size of the United
Kingdom and anchoring it in the North Sea, so that the German
bombers would bomb it rather than the country itself. Another
suggested suspending huge mirrors from balloons in front of cities
so that the bombers, seeing their own reflections flying straight at
them, would take such violent evasive action that they would crash.
A third suggested training sea-gulls to pick the mortar out of walls,
and then hurling waves of mortar-picking birds at German cities
to bring them down in ruins. Many of these, together with more
practical ideas, were thought up and mulled over during evenings
at the local.

The members of a Midlands darts team, during an evening's
game in 1940, suggested that darts should be provided with small
explosive warheads, and that these could be a useful weapon, particularly in trench or close hand-to-hand fighting. As the evening
proceeded and the beer circulated, so the suggestions became less
and less coherent, ending with the poignant appeal that whether
invasion came or not, GHQ should 'Save the Beer'.

The armoured dart idea was, in fact, taken up by GHQ.
Replicas were made and tested at suitable ranges. The dart was

declared an official weapon, but did not go into production. The problem was that it only had a range of twenty feet, and the army authorities felt that, on the whole, a sub-machine gun was probably more effective.

A modern extension of the games-in-pubs concept – and of course of the old tradition of the inn as a literary meeting place – has been the development of poetry and play-reading sessions. Greeted at first with derision, such entertainments have come to form a definite part of the amenities offered by public houses. Some, like the *King's Head* at Islington, were even more ambitious. There, beyond the saloon bar and the grills turning out the inevitable hamburger, was built a small, self-contained theatre. It was based on the Elizabethan model with a stage in the centre, surrounded on three sides by chairs and benches. Thirty or so spectators can see the show at a time, and young directors find it an ideal way of gaining experience, while out-of-work actors are happy to practice their art in exchange for a meal and a pint of bitter. Short plays or adaptions of unusual merit can thus be tried out.

Other pubs provide entertainment of a less 'high-brow' nature. Particularly in city pubs 'drag' evenings and strippers enjoy immense popularity. The tradition of music-making has evolved in turn into what is known as the 'pub rock circuit'. Based on the same principles as pub theatre, the pub rock circuit allows up-and-coming musicians to build up a following, gain vital experience and experiment with new forms in a friendly, appreciative atmosphere.

The mode of the entertainment may have changed, but the spirit and the setting in which it is enjoyed remains the same.

Chapter Ten

Brewers today produce special party cans for those arranging celebrations of one kind or another. But in fact beer has always been closely associated with parties and jollifications of all kinds.

It appeared in the Middle Ages at what was undoubtedly one's first party : baptism. After returning from the church, parents and guests settled down to the serious business of getting through as much Christening ale (four quarts a penny) as possible. Weddings were a natural excuse for more drinking and special Bride ales were produced and distributed among the wedding guests.

Death, of course, also had its special ale. This was called Give ale. Persons wishing to leave for the next, and possibly even more alarming world than the present (the belief in a hell bubbling with boiling oil and scorched with flame was very real), with the best wishes of their friends, would arrange for quantities of Give ale to be distributed so that the deceased could have a cheery farewell.

This was not the same as a wake. The wake was originally a pagan festival mourning the passing of a particular god. The early Christians adopted the custom to include the celebration of a dead saint's birthday. In time, wakes were held whenever somebody died. Sometimes the corpse itself, suitably dressed, would attend the wake as well. The custom was more popular among ignorant people, where early deaths were frequent and there was a need to show, as in a war, that life was not interrupted by death. Wakes were also essentially a Catholic device and disappeared with the arrival of the Protestant faith.

But the practice of Give ale parties still exists. It is not uncommon for a man, especially if he was a convivial type, to leave instructions that his friends are to have, a short while after his death, a party to drink his health and help him on his way, wherever he may be.

The Church was also a great party-giver. Special Church ales were brewed, the church hall stocked with food, and musicians engaged. At the subsequent party, where drinking and dancing were pursued with equal vigour, large quantities of the special Church ale were sold. Sometimes it was brewed on the spot by the church itself. Invariably the malt was given to the church by the wealthier members of the community, and the profits were distributed among the poor.

Then there were Whitsun ales, again specially brewed either by or for the Church, for sale during the Whitsun festivities. Easter, on the other hand, did not fare so well. There were usually no special Easter ales. But in some places at Eastertide, a special ale was brewed and sold to pay the parish clerk. It was known as Clerk ale.

Parish clerks do not appear to have been the sober minded people they are today. Chaucer's Parish Clerk, for example, was an early pop singer, complete with guitar and a repertoire of suitable airs. No doubt his guitar helped the sale of his own Clerk ale.

May Day was always a good excuse for a party. This hangover from pagan days persisted for many years. The raising of the maypole, decorated with hawthorn blossom (long regarded as being associated with the gods – to such an extent that even today it is considered unlucky to bring it into the house), would be a strenuous business, often requiring the help of numerous oxen. Once the pole was up, a celebratory goblet of ale was *de rigeur:*

> The Maypole is up,
> Now give me the cup,
> I'll drink to the garlands around it,
> But first unto those,
> Whose hands did compose,
> The glory of flowers that crown'd it.

During the year there were many other excuses for parties, noticeably after sheep shearing and haymaking. Merrie England lived up to her name. It seems surprising sometimes that there was time to work.

Ales were also named for various other social activities. Foot ale was a liquid fare paid by apprentices when they first got a 'footing' in their new trade. Some employers extended the habit to cover other events. Marriage ale was invented to be drunk whenever an employee announced his or her engagement. This was the origin of the present habit of having a 'whip-round' the office to buy a wedding present. There followed, naturally, Child ales, to celebrate in particular the arrival of the first-born, and Change of Place and Journey ales. Any excuse was seized upon to prolong the five o'clock work-break.

Up until the nineteenth century ale, not tea, was the standard drink for such periods of relaxation. Tea then took over as the natural drink of the work-break, soon renamed the tea-break, and Foot, Marriage, Child and Journey ales vanished before the all-conquering tea-urn and trolley.

But at Christmas-time ale came back once more into popularity.

The end of December has always been a time of rejoicing in the Northern Hemisphere. Earliest man, seeing the beloved sun, to which he owed his life and everything about him, slowly losing its strength and dying throughout the autumn, noted that shortly after what is now known as the winter solstice the patient began to recover and grow daily stronger.

In his relief that his benefactor and giver of life was not in fact going to die, primitive man began to dance and sing. He invited the neighbours to share his happiness. He offered them food and drink. The first party was born.

Though society grew more and more sophisticated, the habit of celebrating the sun's recovery continued. During Roman times it was known as Saturnalia, the first ten days of the sun's revival being devoted to celebrations.

When the Romans finally accepted Christianity as the official state religion, they were careful not to disrupt too violently the old pagan habits. Though Saturnalia was abolished, the celebrations of the birth of Christ were put in its place.

Christmas became established as a religious festival, but still retained its old Saturnalian undertones. For centuries the main activity was the dragging in, on Christmas Eve, of the yule log. The whole community, including soldiers, took part. The log, often a whole tree-trunk, was borne into the hall of the local castle or manor house. It was lit with the charred fragments of last Christmas's brands. As soon as the new log was alight (a symbol still, surely, of the rebirth of the sun) the feasting began.

White bread (a delicacy) and chunks of roasted meat were handed out; to be followed by pies and plums; all washed down by tankards of good strong ale.

A huge candle known as the yule candle lit up the scene. Mummers under the direction of the Lord of Misrule or Master of Merry Disports presented their intricate and symbolic plays. And the ale-jug continued to pass from hand to hand.

There came a change when Queen Victoria married Albert. The Prince Consort had been brought up in the North German tradition of Christmas trees and Father Christmas. He imported the custom to England when he and Victoria began to have children. The custom caught on. Christmas trees replaced the yule log, Father Christmas the mummers; until at the present day, Christmas is an amalgam of different activities: a religious festival, a children's treat and a break from work; while still, at bottom, can be heard the old pagan shout of relief that the sun is not going to die after all.

With drinking, particularly at feast times, came the habit of wishing friends good health. The Romans had their *'Bene te, bene tibi'*, the Saxons their *'Wacht heil'* and *'Drinc heil'*. The Danes, before setting off on an expedition, would drink to each other and the success of their venture. Murders were often committed while the victims drank their host's health from the huge loving cup handed from guest to guest at the end of medieval dinners; as two hands were needed to lift the cup to the lips, the drinker was consequently completely defenceless. A man, creeping up behind him, could easily stab him in the back. To prevent this happening, the person immediately to the drinker's left would rise; and, facing the room, stand guard over his friend.

The custom is still observed in the ceremonious drinking from the loving cup at such functions as livery dinners held by the old guilds of London and other towns. The loving cup passes 'across and across' the table, and as each recipient rises, bows to the opposite number and grasps the loving cup in both hands, his adjacent companion rises, to stand figurative guard over him.

Each generation has its own customs and calls when drinking. The calls vary too from one section of the populace to the other. 'Bottoms Up' and 'Mud in your eye' are recognizable social indications. The modern, laconic 'Cheers' is more universal, more egalitarian; perhaps hereby also an expression of the times.

The careful planner could, until quite recently, have ale at all his meals. Breakfast quite frequently used to consist of ale and bread. In the household accounts of Queen Elizabeth I there are frequent references to the provision of ale for breakfast. Breakfast was then of course a much more substantial meal than today : cold sirloin of beef, ham and other meats were an integral part of the meal. The habit still persists in Australia where the day not infrequently starts with a beef steak and a can of excellent Australian beer.

Between breakfast and the main evening meal came a light meal at noon called 'nunchion'. The word is a distortion of *'noon schenchen* (noon drinking). Again, the chief constituents of the meal were a hunk of bread and a tankard of ale. The word 'luncheon' is a refined distortion of the original word.

Ale was often drunk at dinner. In the higher ranks of society, wine was served together with ale. It was not considered wrong to drink the two side by side. The injunction of not mixing grape and grain did not appear until quite recently and still does not hold in countries like Denmark, where wine, beer and schnapps are drunk simultaneously.

Finally, before we leave the subject of eating and the like, let us remember that at least one man lived entirely on bread and ale, given him by his friends : John Bigg, the seventeenth-century hermit, better known as the Dinton Hermit.

Ale and beer, more than any other liquid except perhaps bath water, seems to bring out the latent singer in the human being. However inhibited or unmusical a person may be, a glass or two of beer will make him believe that what the world really needs is a song. Solos are popular, but even better are community songs with arms linked, and, if possible, some kind of easily executed backwards and forwards movement. The linked arms are not, as one might imagine, a sign of friendship, but an insurance that one will stay upright in the ensuing caper.

Primitive man sang lustily around his camp fires while drinking his home-made brews. No doubt there was a good deal of riotous singing in the Ancient Egyptian *hek* shops before the authorities closed them down. But it was not until the Romans appeared that songs were recorded and handed down. Many were translated and formed the basis of early English drinking songs.

Ballads were popular until the seventeenth century. These long narrative poems were either spoken or sung. Many dealt with the adventures of Sir John Barleycorn, who represented the grain of barley that has to go through all kinds of torture before his friend Thomas Good-Ale comes to his rescue. The farmer tries to kill Sir John and buries him in the ground, but :

> He rested still within the earth,
>   till raine from skies did fall,
> Then he grew up in branches greene,
>   Which sore amaz'd them all.

The whole brewing process is in fact described in detail :

> Then they brought him to the mill,
>   and there they burst his bones,
> The miller swore to murther him
>   betwixt a pair of stones.
>
> Then they took him up againe
>   and serv'd him worse then that;
> For with hot scalding liquor store,
>   they washed him in a Fat.

These ballads about the attempted murder of Sir John Barley-corn originated in the West Country, but were soon adopted by other parts of the British Isles including Scotland. They were more than mere drinking songs, becoming rallying points for expressions of local patriotism. Sir John represented the sturdy countryman who could survive the worst tortures and triumph over all his enemies, even death. For, like many drinking songs, they contained an element of simple philosophy.

Others were of a more homely nature, such as the one entitled simply 'The Parson' which describes the short-comings of a certain clergyman :

> A parson who had the remarkable foible
> Of minding the bottle more than the Bible,

Was deemed by his neighbours to be less perplex'd
In handling a tankard than handling a text.

The ballad goes on to recount how, when the parson was at church
his pigs broke into his cellar, knocked over his barrels and drank
all his beer. So that later on at dinner, when he sent his wife down
to draw the ale, she came back empty-handed. In order to soothe
him, she reminded him of Job, and his patience in the face of mis-
fortune.

'A plague upon Job', cried the priest in his rage,
'That beer, I dare say, was near ten years of age;
But you're a poor ignorant jade like *his* wife;
For Job never had such a cask in his life.'

The ballads eventually gave way to shorter songs, usually
straight exhortations to drink, and yet still containing elements of
philosophical comment :

Drink! Drink!
Drink away!
Never think
On what's to pay!
What is man? A sigh, a vapour.
What is woman? Whitey-brown paper!

This same mixture of enthusiasm for drinking and comment on
life in general is to be found over and over again. It accords with
the somewhat maudlin state drinkers often reach when they
become convinced that they have discovered the secrets of the
universe.

Typical of this type of song is the Yale drinking song 'We are
poor black sheep who have lost our way'. To suitable dirge-like
music the 'gentlemen-songsters off on a spree' admit that they're
'damned from here to eternitee . . .' and ask God to have mercy 'on
such as we. Baa. Baa. Baa.'

Finally, drinking songs often have a social context. The Eton
Boating Song, though not perhaps originally intended as a drinking song, evokes a certain social strata, just as 'Knees up, Mother

Brown' brings another to mind. The 'Lambeth Walk', sung first in public houses south of the River Thames, became almost a national anthem during the Second World War. And what would New Year's Eve be like without 'Auld Lang Syne'?

Chapter Eleven

Beer can be found in the most unexpected places. Though it is natural to assume that soldiers might be fond of it, it comes as a surprise to learn that as long ago as 1512 it was considered an essential part of an army's equipment. There were complaints from the army in France about a shortage of this natural drink; soldiers were being forced to drink wine or cider. The former, it was claimed, burned their stomachs; the latter made them sick.

Beer arrived in India with the first British regiments. Soon there was such a demand for the drink that the brewers made a special study of the best kind of beer for the hot climate. The answer was India Pale Ale. It can still be bought in English pubs, though very few realize today that this was once an exclusive army drink.

In one form or another beer has been carried with the stores and ammunition on almost every operation carried out by the British Army. It has accompanied expeditions to the hottest tropics and coldest arctic climates. It has been carried through claustrophobic jungles and over the most rarefied of mountain peaks. Wherever the army has marched, somewhere, on mule, limber or pack, the faithful reminder of home has followed.

But it was not merely as a welcome relief to the fatigues of war that beer followed the troops. It was also used as a medicine.

Towards the end of the eighteenth century a chemist called Jackson, working under the instructions of the Admiralty, produced a dehydrated malt. It could be stored in ships and took up much less space than the bulky casks. By adding water, beer could be produced.

This was an early example of an instant drink, even though it took two days for the liquid to settle properly. Nevertheless, on journeys that took from six to eighteen months or more, two days' wait was not such an ordeal.

Captain Cook took the special malt on his journey to New Zealand and Australia. It provided both a welcome reminder of home and was a useful defence against scurvy. In 1779 the Admiralty directed that all ships on foreign service should carry the new malt.

Other experiments were carried out with dehydrated malts but were not successful. And when first lemon and then lime took over as the main protectors against scurvy, the malt process was abandoned.

It was from seeing English sailors drinking their lime that the Americans called them 'limeys', a name that is still in use. Had the anti-scurvy malt been more successful, no doubt our American 'cousins' would have called us 'malties'.

The need to produce beer for troops serving overseas became acute again in the 1939-45 War. Churchill, learning that troops in the Far East were rationed to three bottles of beer a month, suggested that they should, somehow or another, be given more. George Brown, the head brewer of Trumans' London Brewery, was serving with the London Scottish Regiment in Italy at the time. Recalled suddenly, he was promoted to Lieutenant Commander RNVR (special branch) and, thus sanctified, sent to Canada to supervise the assembly of a brewing unit on the Royal Naval amenity ship, *M.V. Menestheus*. She was a funnel passenger ship converted for use by the NAAFI, and carried all kinds of comforts for the troops.

The brewing unit consisted of two brewers, two petty officers, eight ratings and five Chinese stewards. Distilled sea-water, malt extract, hop concentrate and yeast were used. The resulting drink was known as Davy Jones Ale and sold at ninepence (4p) a pint. It was supplied to troops operating in the Pacific and Indian Ocean areas, and was a welcome addition to the statutory three bottles a month. A special poster was produced, which proclaimed :

Something from the OLD COUNTRY ! . . .
A Breath from BRITAIN ! ! . . .
ENGLISH MILD ALE
brewed in
Davy Jones Brewery
'The World's Only Floating Brewery !'

On sale at all bars with unlimited supply, 9d pint
Operated by Navy, Army and Air Force Institutes
Sponsored by Board of Admiralty.

Another beer-supplying effort, but this time unofficial, occurred
during the Normandy campaign in 1944. For although the invad-
ing troops were plentifully supplied with arms and ammunition,
there was a certain deficiency in their stocks of beer.

Some of the Spitfire pilots of the 2nd Tactical Air Force decided
to remedy this state of affairs. By a careful modification of the
bomb-racks beneath the Spitfires' wings, it was found that barrels
of beer could be slung there instead. Operation Depth Charge
Fitment came into being. Spitfires landing on the advance landing
strips in France would unload their barrel 'bombs' before taking
on real bombs. Whenever a fresh consignment of beer arrived,
word spread quickly, and there was keen competition to acquire
one of these Spitfire barrels.

Strong and Company of Romsey produced the barrels and the
beer. So accurate and precise were the sketches showing the fit-
ments for these special 'depth charges' that they were sent up to the
Air Ministry by mistake. Only a last minute telephone call pre-
vented them being passed by the Modifications Committee and
becoming standard, if somewhat outlandish, RAF equipment.

The belief that beer has useful medical properties – especially for
the fighting man – persists to modern times. In the Second World
War Guinness was a standard medicine for wounded soldiers. In
many hospitals, a bottle of Guinness a day was an accepted part of
the treatment for the convalescent soldier.

Though beer was prized by the Army, it was not regarded so
highly by the Royal Navy. It is true that ships would carry tuns of
beer in their holds, but these were usually for the soldiers who
might be on board.

The Navy's stimulus was always spirits. It used to be neat spirits,
usually rum. But Admiral Vernon, when in command of the fleet
in 1740, issued an order that the rum ration should be mixed with
water. The order did not increase the admiral's popularity. Not
that he cared. He would stride about the deck of his flagship whenever the sea was rough, with an old grogram cloak made of un-
treated silk and mohair across his shoulders. 'There goes old Grog

himself,' the sailors would mutter. And they christened his watered drink 'grog' too.

The youngest of the Services, the RAF, has not adopted an 'official' drink, but during the hectic days of 1940, young pilots would return from yet another aerial fight to find a modest bottle of beer awaiting them.

The belief that ale or beer has medicinal properties is of long standing. Special medicated ales were brewed in the sixteenth and seventeenth centuries for all kinds of illnesses. One was called Panala. Its manufacturers claimed, as with other patent medicines, that it was a universal cure for every known disease, and that it could be safely taken by any 'Age, Sex or Constitution'. 'Buttered Beere' was considered good for coughs and shortness of breath. Besides beer, it contained fresh butter, sugar, grated ginger and two yolks of egg per tankard. Almost a meal in itself. Thomas Cogan's 'Haven of Health', a mysterious brew, was supposed to cure gout. As part of the cure consisted of not drinking wine, a major cause of gout, it was remarkably successful.

Then there was Dr Butler's celebrated medical ale, that was on sale at inns for at least two centuries. Its manufacture was relatively simple. A thin canvas bag containing senna pods, polypedrum, sarsaparilla and other herbs, was allowed to hang in nine or ten gallons of ale. After three or four days the bag was removed, and the liquid then bottled. The inns that sold Butler's Ale carried a signboard with a painting of the good doctor himself upon it. It was said to be good both for the stomach and the lungs, and a guard against indigestion and colds; a claim that was probably true, considering the medical ingredients contained in the bag.

Specific ales were produced for specific illnesses. Thus in 1744 a brown ale called Stitch was considered an effective cure for consumption. Even as late as 1886 a form of cough mixture was made of malt and water. It had to be boiled up quickly, stirring all the time, until the mixture was as thick as treacle. The unfortunate invalid was expected to swallow a dessert spoon of the concoction three times a day.

One enterprising physician, a certain Dr Solas Dodd, put forward in 1753 the suggestion that before operating on a patient the victim should be given a quart of warm ale, suitably laced with henbane, hemlock and other drugs. Once asleep, any amount of

amputating could be done without the patient even stirring. It is
not recorded whether this early and ingenious form of anaesthetic
was ever used.

Health-giving beer has been used not only internally, but exter-
nally as well. Some while ago, women discovered that if they
washed their hair in beer, the result was rather pleasing. Their
hair became soft and springy. It acquired a sheen that it did not
possess before. Hairdressers were not slow to adopt the idea. Today,
a variety of hair lotions with a beer foundation are on sale.

In all events the taking of ale was always considered good for
health, and a recipe for a long and active life, as the following
gravestone epitaph shows :

> Here John Randal lies
> Who counting of his Tale
> Lived threescore years and Ten,
> Such vertue was in ale.
> Ale was his meat,
> Ale was his drink.
> Ale did his heart revive,
> And if he could have drunk his ale
> He still had been alive.

To which it might be added that the record for the longest-living
Englishman is held by an ale-drinker called Henry Jenkins, some-
time butler to Lord Conyers, and a keen thatcher and salmon-
fisher, who died in 1670 at the respectable age of 165.

It might be thought that it would be a short step from using ale
and beer as medicine to using it as an adjunct to cooking. Wine,
after all, has been used throughout the rest of Europe for centuries,
to add a new dimension to food. Yet, apart from one or two special
dishes, neither ale nor beer has, so far, been greatly used in cooking. There are a number of possible reasons. Good food was for a
long time the prerogative of the upper classes, and since the
Norman invasion the French influence was uppermost. Wine, not
ale, was used in cookery.

Spices and herbs were already much in use, as a means of pre-
serving meat. The town of Saffron Walden, for instance, gets its
name from the fields of saffron that used to be cultivated there. The

piquant taste of spices did not mix well with the more solid taste of ale. Wine, perhaps because of its higher acid content, could overcome the spice element.

Then, after the Black Death, with the scarcity of labour and the high wages commanded by the surviving farm labourers, farmers went over to beef farming. A herd of cattle required less labour than a field of wheat. The quality of meat therefore improved. There was no longer any need, as in more southern countries, to disguise its shortcomings with elaborate sauces. Meat could be eaten for its own sake and taste.

Finally, from Anglo-Saxon times onwards, drinking has been a serious business. Not for the inhabitants of these islands has been the appreciative sip of an exotic wine. Ale and beer should be downed in large quantities and as frequently as possible. It was too revered a drink to be squandered on cooking; and often it was too strong. The Earl of Leicester, writing to Lord Burleigh from Hatfield, where Queen Elizabeth I was staying, complained that 'there was not one drop of good drink for her there. We were fain to send to London and Kenilworth and divers other places where ale was; her own bere was so strong as there was no man able to drink it.'

So for centuries ale and beer were hardly considered as a possible ingredient for food. The only exception appears to have been welsh rabbit. This odd cheese dish is in fact basically a cheese and beer dish. All that has happened is that instead of eating the cheese and drinking the ale separately and cold, they are taken together, hot.

The only other dish with a beer basis that is at all well-known in Britain is the Belgian national dish *carbonnades flamandes,* or beef stewed in beer.

Yet almost every recipe using wine as a basis can be made with beer. Indeed, a whole menu can be made up : Scots pheasant soup (flavoured with sweet stout) can be followed by lobster in beer sauce as a fish course. For meat, there is a large variety of dishes besides the famous *carbonnades* to choose from; including roast leg of lamb cooked in half a pint of stout. Dessert, surprisingly enough, presents no difficulty at all : if it is Christmas-time, the flavour of Christmas pudding can be improved with the addition of half a pint of light ale. For the rest of the year there is a choice of peach trifle flavoured with lager or apple dumplings and brown ale, while waffles, cheesecakes and even banana fritters can be improved, it is claimed, by the addition of light ale. And, of course, there is always welsh rabbit to finish with.

A huge variety of drinks could accompany this meal : pale ale, mild ale, stout, porter, or any number of cask or bottled beers. Finally, a cup of old-fashioned wassail complete with cinnamon, nutmeg and apple rings, can bring this completely beer-oriented meal to an undoubtedly welcome close.

If this sounds daunting enough, let us remember the past and the huge repasts served up to our ancestors. It is recorded that when George Neville was made Archbishop of York in the reign of Edward IV, a huge meal was prepared consisting of, among other things, 104 oxen, 400 swans, 1,000 sheep, 2,000 pigs and 300 tuns of ale, one tun being 252 gallons. Although this gigantic meal was undoubtedly intended for a large number of people, the good trenchermen of the past would have worked their way through the tentative all-beer menu outlined above with the greatest of ease.

If they could, then surely so can we.

Part Three

The Money Game

Chapter Twelve

Once made, ale must be sold. A very early and still popular form of salesmanship was the sign post outside inns.

The simple bush or branch of a tree stuck on a pole that used to tell travellers where the early alehouse was situated soon gave way to more sophisticated types of inn signs. Signs were not restricted to inns. At a time when less than 5 per cent of the population could read and write, signs were the quickest way traders could tell the public what they were selling. Every trade had its sign. Meat sellers would display heads of animals, many of them beautifully carved. Horses' heads carved from wood and painted gold can still be seen outside French butchers' shops where horsemeat is sold. Hosiers usually hung out a huge wooden leg. When scissors were invented they took over from the knife displayed by cutlers. Booksellers were known by the curious sign of a colophon, the ornamental tail-piece clipped onto the end of old books that gave the title of the book, name of author and other information usually found today on the title page.

Most of these signs disappeared when the population became more literate. But some, the more bizarre, have continued to this day. The pawnbrokers' three golden balls are still to be found. The sign was in fact the arms of Lombardy and was brought here in 1299 by moneylenders from that country. The barbers' red-and-white pole can be seen for decorative purposes outside barbers' shops. The red signified blood, the white, bandages. Barbers originally had some medical knowledge and could treat customers for cuts and abrasions.

At one time signs became so numerous that they blocked the view in the streets and became a danger to passers-by, not infrequently crashing down during a storm. Attempts were made to

Ancient Alehouse.

restrict their use; a tax was even imposed on them. They eventually disappeared of their own accord when shops began to display the names of the owner rather than the nature of the goods to be bought inside.

The inn sign, however, survived; mainly because in 1393 the innkeepers in London were obliged by law to display a sign. The custom was taken up in other parts of the country. This law accounts for the strange incongruity of certain old signs, such as the *Fleece and Seven Stars.* Historians might try to find some rational explanation for this odd mixture, but in fact the truth probably was that an innkeeper trading at an inn called the *Fleece,* a popular name, went into partnership with another innkeeper running the *Seven Stars.* As neither would wish to give up the name of his original house, the new inn would combine the two original names and be called the *Fleece and Seven Stars.*

At first the signs were simple representations of animals and birds found in the farms and countryside: fox, cow, hen or pig. The effigy of the chosen beast, highly coloured, would be fixed in a hoop suspended at the end of the ale-post. In a stiff breeze these effigies would swing joyfully. A particularly popular sign was the cock in a hoop, and people coming out of such alehouses were, it seemed to onlookers, 'cock-a-hoop' themselves.

Simple country animal names continue to this day, although their derivation is not always as straightforward as it might seem. The bull is an obvious sign; but the *Bull and Gate*, which stood in Holborn, was a derivation of 'Boulogne Gates'. These once stood at the entrance to Boulogne and were brought to Kent after Henry VIII's army had stormed the city.

The cock, without its hoop, has survived too. There used to be two inns at Stony Stratford on the main road from the North to London. One was called the *Cock* and the other the *Bull*. They were staging inns, where the stage-coaches changed horses on their journeys to London with letters and travellers. While the horses were being changed – the tired ones being kept at the inns to be fed and rested until required on the return journey, and the new and sprightly ones harnessed and made ready – the passengers would gather in the inn's parlour for a drink.

During the middle part of the eighteenth century the innkeepers of these two inns happened to be devoted rumourmongers. As there was almost continuous war with France at the time, they used to spell out elaborate tales of disaster in the field. Alarmed, the travellers would arrive in London with these tales. At first they were believed, but it was soon discovered that anybody who had stopped at either the *Cock* or the *Bull* at Stony Stratford tended to be primed with misleading and alarming information. 'Just another Cock-and-Bull story,' people would say as they listened to the latest and most unlikely tale brought in by the travellers. The expression has become part of the English language.

As time went on, the simple effigy sign gave way to more elaborate signs usually painted on boards. These were extremely diverse and of differing origins. Some prolonged the country theme : the *Plough and the Packhorse* replacing the *Hen and the Pig*. Others touched on the business of brewing and agriculture in general : the *Barleycorn* was a favourite name. So was the *Wheatsheaf*, the *Fleece* and the *Woolpack*. The *Weavers Arms* celebrated the wealth to be obtained from the wool trade, and the *Blacksmith's Arms* is self-explanatory.

In many parts of the country, inns would take their names from the houses of the local gentry. Sometimes they were even situated in those houses. Or the inn would be named, as a mark of respect, after the most important family in the district, the local squire allowing the inn to use his coat of arms as a sign. Often, indeed, he would insist on it.

Thus sprang up a whole series of heraldic signs. The *Crown* and its various derivations has always been a favourite. Even today it heads the popularity list with 1,099 pubs named after it. Next comes the *Red Lion,* the heraldic symbol of Scotland. Popular too are the *Golden Lions* (of England) and the *White Lions* (found in the arms of the Dukes of Norfolk). There are *Black Lions* (from the arms of the De Crespigny family) and even *Blue Lions* (of the Mildmay family).

Then there are the *King's Heads.* No less than 460 inns have this sign. The kings themselves vary, but the signs are very much alike. *Queen's Heads* are equally numerous. Queen Elizabeth I is a particular favourite, as is Queen Victoria, particularly as she was when an ageing widow in black, with a flowing mantilla on her head, and a crown perched on top.

Sometimes the aristocratic derivation is not so easy to trace. The *Lygon Arms,* at Broadway, is a straightforward family sign, but what of the *Eagle and Child*? This does not refer, at least directly, to a legend, but is in fact the crest of the Earls of Derby. It is true that the crest comes from a family legend that one of the Earl of Derby's ancestors was found in an eagle's nest (as improbably as Moses was found in the bull-rushes) and adopted. But the reason it was used as an inn sign was as a mark of respect to the family.

An interesting sign is the *Talbot.* It depicts an animal that no longer exists. The talbot was a huge white hound used in medieval times for hunting. It is now extinct, although it is possible that the modern breed of hounds may have descended from it. Two white talbots form part of the arms of Talbot, the Earls of Shrewsbury, and this is the reason for the use of the sign. A popular and some-what irreverent version of the stately talbot is the cheeky *Spotted Dog.*

Then there is the whole group of *New Inns.* They originated at the time of Elizabeth I when the government put into operation a daring and novel development scheme. In order to make the main roads safer and to provide shelter for the night, it decreed that new inns were to be built at certain fixed intervals along the roads. The distance between each was to be nineteen miles, this being the amount of mileage a loaded pack-mule could be expected to cover in a day. *New Inns* of Elizabethan origin – or at least built on their sites – can still be found, particularly in Devon; and the distance between them is remarkably close to nineteen miles.

There are a number of signs celebrating specific events. One of the most popular and romantic is the *Royal Oak*. This commemorates Charles II's escape after the battle of Worcester in 1651 when he hid in a tree at Boscobel. Innkeepers had a particular bias towards the Cavaliers; perhaps because the Roundheads were so often abstainers. The innkeeper of the *George Inn* at Broadwindsor in Dorset, by the name of Rice Jones, was no exception. He kept watch while Charles II and his party finally made their escape from the country. When the King returned at the Restoration, he presented Mr Rice Jones with a magnificent carved oak bedstead. *Royal Oak* inns, celebrating the King's lucky escape, sprang up all over the country after the Restoration. There are still 750 of them in existence.

A strange sign is the *Silent Woman* or the *Good Woman* as it is sometimes called, which is found on the Continent as well as in this country. It often depicts a decapitated woman carrying her head in her arm. No completely satisfactory explanation for this sign has been put forward. It may be a reference to the *heed*less (which became *head*-less) virgins who had no oil for lamps, or to the old belief that women could only stop talking if you cut their heads off. Perhaps it is something much older and more primitive, a throw-back to witches, warlocks and black magic.

A woman also figures in the *Load of Mischief* which depicts a woman astride a man's back. He is also supporting a magpie and a monkey. He has a chain and padlock, labelled 'wedlock', round his neck. There is a pair of cuckold's horns on the roof of the house on the left of the sign, while to the right is depicted the prosperous mansion of 'S. Gripe, Pawnbroker'. The sign was painted by Hogarth to pay for his drinks at an old alehouse of that name that stood in Oxford Street.

There have been a number of variations of the *Load of Mischief*. Some had the words 'Drawn by Experience, engraved by Sorrow' on them. Sometimes the following couplet would accompany it:

> A monkey, a magpie and a wife,
> Is the true emblem of strife.

Like the *Silent Woman* this sign is also found in France. It is called *Le Trio de Malice* and shows a woman and a monkey but the magpie is replaced by a cat.

Popular heroes were often depicted on inn signs. There are any number of *Duke of Wellingtons.* The *Marquis of Granby* is another popular sign. It is in honour of John Manners, Marquis of Granby (1721-1770). The sign invariably shows the Marquis bald. This was because, when leading a cavalry charge against the French, a shot carried off his hat and wig and the great man was revealed to be completely bald. Undaunted, he continued to charge. The French, perhaps alarmed at this unusual sight, fled.

The Adam and Eve of the arms of the Fruiterers' Company have been in existence since the sixteenth century; there is an *Adam and Eve,* appropriately enough, in Paradise, Gloucestershire. And there is a *Rose Revived* at Burford near Oxford, so called not because of the flower on its sign but because Mr Rose revived the pub in the 1950s.

As time went on so the inn signs became more and more elaborate. The single boards that followed the original hoops became in turn elaborate constructions protruding ten or fifteen feet over the road. Sometimes these poles were so heavy that they pulled away part of the tavern wall and crashed down onto the roadway itself, holding up traffic for hours.

Conditions got so bad that in the reign of Henry V the authorities ordered that stakes bearing inn signs were not to extend more than seven feet over the highway. The penalty for breaking this decree was a forty-shilling fine.

Nevertheless, the stakes continued to extend until it was necessary to support the further end by another pole or pillar. Thus the signboard spanning the whole road came into existence. By the eighteenth century these archway signs were a common sight in both towns and villages throughout Britain. The usual kind was a fairly simple structure extending from the first-floor window level across the street to an upright built like a gallows. The sign itself swung either from the middle or the far side of the horizontal bar. A typical example of such a spanning signboard was to be found at the *Black Boy* at Chelmsford.

The most elaborate one was undoubtedly at the *White Hart Inn* at Scole in Norfolk. It was a huge construction tall as the inn itself.

It spanned the road from one verge to the other, and the arch was high enough to allow a fully loaded coach to pass easily under it. It was remarkable for the enormously complicated carvings with which it was decorated. Besides a number of beautifully carved harts, there was Diana with her bow watching her hounds attacking Actæon as he turns into a hart himself. Other mythological or biblical scenes included Charon ferrying a witch across the Styx, Neptune riding the waves on the back of a dolphin, and Jonah escaping from the whale's mouth.

By the middle of the eighteenth century, these spanning sign posts, though attractive, had become so troublesome that a series of Acts of Parliament were passed forbidding sign posts to project at all over the highway. From then onwards they had to either be fixed to the wall or project outwards on private land only.

Although the practical usefulness of inn signs has largely vanished owing to the increasing literacy of the population, they continue to exist as essential parts of the decor of the inn or public house. The old favourites are as popular as ever; and new ones are still being added. After the Korean War a public house called the *Gloster* put up a new sign : it showed a soldier of the Gloucestershire Regiment fighting at the Imjim River in 1951.

More recently still, the space age has begun to be represented. There is the *Flying Saucer*, the *Astronaut,* even the *Telstar.* That old favourite of the nursery rhyme, the cow that jumped over the moon, is also depicted on the sign of an inn called the *Spotted Cow.* The self-satisfied animal is shown with an astronaut's medallion round its neck, inscribed 'First over the Moon'.

Chapter Thirteen

It is not always an easy matter to determine the origin of an inn sign. The *Pig and Whistle* is a case in point. It is said to be a distortion of *Peg and Wassail,* a reference to the peg tankards of Saxon times. But this is only one solution among many. Some are extremely ingenious, although far-fetched. It could come from the pyx (a silver container used at mass) and the housel (consecrated wafer), the pig and whistle being a ribald medieval equivalent. There is a carving of a pig, or rather a sow, blowing a whistle at Winchester Cathedral. An even more obscure theory claims that it comes from the old Danish-Saxon phrase *'Pige Washael'* which meant 'Hail to the Virgin.' Oddly enough, less than a dozen pubs are called the *Pig and Whistle.*

Another confusing name is the *Cat and the Fiddle.* Here again there is a possible religious significance, for at Beverley Minster there is an old carving showing a cat playing a fiddle. On the other hand, it could be a distortion of Caton Fidele, who defended Calais and like other heroes had inns named after him. Or the name may simply have been chosen because people liked the nursery rhyme allusion.

The mispronunciation of foreign or difficult words is said to be behind the names of a number of inns. The popular *Elephant and Castle* could be a distortion of the *Infanta Castille,* a ship that moored in the Thames when the original inn was built. The innkeeper called his house after the visiting ship, perhaps hoping the ship's crew would make it their local. While the *Stewponey* near Stourbridge was a distortion of the town of Estepona in Spain. The first innkeeper had fought in Spain at the time of Queen Anne, married a girl from Estepona and called his inn after her home town.

7 Pimlico Lodge, 1848, drawn by John Elliot. The Stag Brewery of Elliot Watney and Co. adjoins the house.

8 The Stag Brewery, 1880; No. 2 vat house and store.

9 'A Brewery Yard'. Painted c. 1825 by Dean Wolstenholme.

Even more confusing is the *Bag o'Nails,* a linguistic distortion of the Bacchanals, the mythological drinkers of the Greek sagas. The *Goat and Compass* on the other hand is a straight corruption of 'God Encompass Us', the motto of the Puritans, the distortion being used ironically by their opponents.

The *Mytton and Mermaid* at Atcham near Shrewsbury derives from the mixture of a real person, John Mytton, an eccentric local squire, and the distortion of a 'mere' maid he was said to have pursued. The *Mermaid* in its own right was long a popular sign. The famous *Mermaid Tavern* in Fleet Street was in existence in 1464; and in a work on choosing inn names published in 1631, one of the characters suggests that a mermaid would pull in the customers. It is not known whether this was a reference to the dangerous siren of the seas, or a reference to girls in general. Perhaps both.

The most incomprehensible inn name to any except Welsh-speaking people is probably the *Gwalchmai* in Anglesey. It is, in fact, a kind of sea bird.

Sarcastic signs include the *Honest Lawyer,* a headless figure, and the *World Turned Upside Down.* Here hounds are ridden by foxes in pursuit of man; and a pig is quietly killing a butcher.

Perhaps most interesting of all are the *Five Alls.* There are a number of versions of this sign and they date from the eighteenth century. Originally there were four 'Alls' :

> The Ploughman works for All,
> The Parson prays for All,
> The Soldier fights for All,
> And the Farmer pays for All.

To these were added a cryptic fifth :

> The Devil who takes All.

Other versions show a king – in Rowlandson's time a caricature of George IV – ('I rule All'); a bishop ('I pray for All'); a lawyer ('I plead for All'); a soldier ('I fight for All') and a labourer ('I pay for All'). Later the labourer was dropped in favour of a heavily-shackled tax-payer.

Occasionally an inn's name will pay a compliment to a lady.

The *Bell Sauvage* of Ludgate Hill was so called after Belle Savage, its first and reputedly attractive if somewhat wanton proprietress.

Most mysterious of inn signs is perhaps the *Green Man*. Four hundred years ago, the Lord Mayor's Shows had green or wild men mixing in with the processions. They had a double role : to entertain with somersaults and fireworks, and at the same time to make a way through the crowds for the Lord Mayor and other VIPs. In fact they were both buskers and policemen.

The Green Man himself goes a great deal further back in history. He is usually dressed entirely in green leaves and he often carries a branch and wields a cudgel. It has been suggested that he is the last remnant of the original inhabitants of these islands, that poetic, civilized world that was banished to the mountains in the west with the invasion of the practical Anglo-Saxons. The hobgoblins, the leprechauns, the pixies and the green men were in reality the small dark-skinned Celts who took refuge in the wilder parts of the land and raided Saxon farms in search of livestock, women and sometimes babies. It is not for nothing that the legends about the 'little folk' are to be found mostly in the west, where the Celts held out longest against the invaders.

But another theory takes the origin of the Green Man even further back in time, to prehistoric times when even man himself had not yet appeared. The earth was then the domain of the spirit world. The Green Man was one of these daemons, perhaps the great Pan himself.

So perhaps of all the inn signs, the *Green Man* is the oldest, giving respect still to the wild cloven-hoofed god who once ruled this land.

The art of producing inn signs reached its peak in the eighteenth century. They were still useful enough to be needed yet society was sophisticated enough to wish for something better than a crude daub.

The best sign painters were the coach painters. These craftsmen made their living from painting the coach panels of the wealthy. The subjects on these panels could be the armorial crest of the family concerned; but equally delicate subjects, *à la Watteau,* were popular : young lovers playing with swings in idealized parks, or walking coyly hand in hand through formal gardens.

As a side-line these experienced artisans would paint the local inn sign either for payment in cash or kind, or as part of a coach panel contract for the local squire or landlord.

But it was not always so. Quite often the sign painter could only paint one sign, and would repeat it over and over again regardless of the needs of the inn in question.

Queen Elizabeth I was a popular subject in her own lifetime for patriotic sign painters. Some of their efforts, however, did not satisfy the Queen's touchy sense of her own appearance. So offended was she by some of the results that she issued a Royal Proclamation which roundly declared 'that portraits of herself, made by unskilful and common painters, should be knocked in pieces, and cast into the fire.' It is not recorded how many of her portraits were in fact knocked to pieces and burned, but to make quite sure that her commands were obeyed, the imperious yet feminine Queen had an officially-approved portrait of herself made, and gave instructions that this was to be used as a model. To this day, inn signs depicting Good Queen Bess are all alike, and derive from this sixteenth-century portrait.

By the eighteenth century much of the business of painting inn signs had passed from the craftsman to the professional painter. To many painters, struggling to achieve fame, it was their means of earning a livelihood; the equivalent today of a 'serious' painter turning to commercial art to keep himself and his family alive.

There was even a market devoted entirely to 'off-the-peg' signs. Here a potential buyer could walk among the stalls and choose a suitable sign for his inn, shop or business. Artists would spend the evenings designing signs and bring them to the market early in the morning. It was held in Harp Lane, and continued until Parliament passed an act during George III's reign forbidding shops to display signs. There were not enough innkeepers looking for new sign boards to support the Harp Market and it closed down.

In 1761, an exhibition of English art was opened in the Great Hall at Spring Gardens. To get in, the patrons had to buy a catalogue illustrated by Hogarth. This was the origin of the yearly Royal Academy exhibitions. At the same time a burlesque of this show opened at nearby Bow Street. The paintings were said to be by the Society of Sign-Painters, and showed 'specimens of the native genius of the nation' – a dig at the somewhat portentous claims of the 'serious' exhibition at Spring Gardens.

It was at this spoof exhibition that Hogarth, happy enough to contribute to both, showed his famous inn sign 'A Man with a Load of Mischief'.

Even when the Royal Academy came into being, its members were not above painting the occasional inn sign. Wale, the Royal Academy's first librarian and professor of painting, produced a portrait of Shakespeare for an inn situated at the north-east corner of Little Russell Street, Drury Lane, for the sum of £500, including the frame.

Penny and Catton, both early members of the Royal Academy, painted inn signs. David Cox painted the sign for the *Royal Oak* at Bettws-y-Coed in North Wales. George Morland painted quite a number of signs in and around London, usually for the inns he liked to frequent. Millais was said to have painted the sign for the *George and Dragon* at Hayes in Kent. More recently, Mervyn Peake, when he lived in Sark in 1950, painted the inn sign for the *Dixcart Hotel.*

From real inns to fictitious ones is a short step. English literature is full of allusions to ale, beer and the welcome places where they can be found.

Chaucer's pilgrims were ever quenching their thirst as they made their way to Canterbury. The Cook was an expert on London ale. The Miller, who was drunk before he even started his tale, asked the company to forgive him. It is, he says, all the fault of the 'ale of Southwerk'.

Shakespeare's plays are full of drinking. The most famous scenes are perhaps those where Falstaff takes his ease with garrulous Dame Quickly in his favourite inn. This was a real inn, the *Boar's Head* in Eastcheap. It was destroyed in the Great Fire of London in 1660 but later rebuilt. It was owned for some time by the Church, having been bequeathed by a dying landlord to St Michael's Church, Crooked Lane, to provide a living for the chaplain. Vestry meetings were held in these unusual, if agreeable, surroundings. The *Boar's Head* ceased to be an inn in about 1790.

In Gammer Gurton's 'Needle', attributed to a sixteenth-century Cambridge don called William Stevenson, are the lines:

> Back and side go bare, go bare,
> Both foot and hand go cold;

But belly, God send thee good ale enough,
Whether it be new or old.

Even gloomy Milton managed one line for ale in his poem 'L'Allegro' : 'Then to the spicy nut-brown ale'.

Inns appear in both Fielding's *Joseph Andrews* and Goldsmith's *The Vicar of Wakefield*. In both cases the parson heroes enjoy the company to be found at the inn. Fielding's Parson Adams, that grave and erudite man, makes his first appearance at an inn, while the worldly Vicar of Wakefield calls at an inn with a group of strolling players.

Of all writers, however, Dickens was perhaps the greatest describer of inns. All of them are said to have been modelled, like much of his work, on real places. Inns seem to appear in every book, whether they are serious ones like *David Copperfield, Barnaby Rudge* or *Martin Chuzzlewit,* or comedies like *The Pickwick Papers.* It is at an inn that Pickwick, Winkle and Snodgrass finally find the absconding Tupman. It is at an inn too that Pickwick first meets Sam Weller. While in *Our Mutual Friend* occurs the jolly jingle :

Who comes here?
A Grenadier.
What does he want?
A pot of beer.

Which brings to mind that other verse about a grenadier, this time found on a tombstone in a Winchester cemetery :

Here sleeps in peace a Hampshire grenadier,
Who caught his death by drinking cold small beer,
Soldiers, take heed from this untimely fall,
And when you're hot, drink strong, or not at all.

Thomas Hughes, the author of *Tom Brown's Schooldays,* wrote that though life isn't all beer and skittles, something of the sort must form a good part of a man's education. The first half of his pronouncement has become part of the language. The second half is the more thought-provoking and interesting. Beer and skittles, representing as they do the lighter side of life, are very much a part of English life. There seems to be no occupation, serious or frivolous, where at least beer does not appear. Skittles? Well, that could be thought of as a symbol of what happens when beer is drunk.

Ale and inns have produced their crop of proverbs and sayings : 'A man knows his companion in a long journey and a little inn;' 'He goes not out of his way that goes to a good inn;' 'Good ale is meat, drink and cloth;' but also 'Good ale will make a cat speak.' While a longer and more complex one states :

> He that buys land buys many stones;
> He that buys flesh buys many bones;
> He that buys eggs buys many shells;
> He that buys good ale buys nothing else.

A minor form of artistic effort can be seen in sign-rhymes found in inns. These are very varied. Sometimes they present a commentary on the landlord's other occupation. Thus an innkeeper who was also a barber had this piece of verse printed under the barber's pole that decorated his inn :

> Roam not from Pole to Pole,
>   But step in here,
> Where naught excels the shaving
>   But the Beer.

Alternatively they are a means of telling customers that a particular inn is the best in the district. Thus there used to be an inn on the old Bath Road called the *White Horse*. Nearby were four other inns, the *Bear,* the *Angel,* the *Ship* and the *Three Cups*. A customer, said to be a literary man, composed the following ditty in exchange for his drink :

> My *White Horse* shall beat the *Bear,*
>   And make the *Angel* fly,
> Shall turn the *Ship* quite bottom up,
>   And drink the *Three Cups* dry.

These lines were duly painted under the sign of the *White Horse*.

What action, if any, the four other inns took in this rustic advertising battle, is not recorded.

Sometimes the sign-rhyme would contain punning references to the innkeeper's name. Beer and punning have always seemed to be companions. Usually the puns were quite simple, but they could be almost excruciatingly complex. There was once an inn half-way up Richmond Hill, at Douglas, Isle of Man, owned by a landlord called Abraham Benjamin Lowe. His sense of punning and flair for advertisement led to this elaborate rhyme :

> I'm Abraham B. Lowe, and half-way up the hill.
> If I were higher up, what's funnier still,
> I'm yet Abe below. So come, drink up your fill
> Of porter, ale, wine, spirits, what you will.
> Step in, my friend, I pray no further go,
> My prices, like myself, are always low.

Simplest, and probably most effective of these advertising rhyme-signs were the couplets painted on each side of a signboard of an inn standing on the edge of Dartmoor. A traveller approaching the dark and frightening moor could read :

> Before the wild moor you venture to pass,
> Pray step within and take a glass.

So he would go in, have his beer and, thus fortified, set off across the moor. On his return journey, he would catch sight of the same inn; but now, as he approached it, he would see the reverse side of the signboard :

> Now that the bleak moor you've safely got over,
> Do stop awhile your spirits to recover.

Chapter Fourteen

Until quite recently, brewing beer was essentially a family concern. The first brewers were humble cottagers; and even when brewing developed into a large-scale, nationwide enterprise, it still remained in the control, for the most part, of single families. John Galsworthy's 'Forsyte Saga' might equally well have been built around a successful brewing family. A number of these brewing families have become household names.

The Watney family is fairly representative.

No one knows where the first Watney came from; for there is no record of any such name prior to 1705. But there are various family legends to account for the first Watney's sudden appearance at that date. His Christian name was Daniel, but it might more appropriately have been Adam, for all subsequent Watneys are descended from him. Indeed, even today, there is only one family of that name in existence. It was said that he was a foundling abandoned on Wimbledon Common; it being a fairly usual practice in those days for private coaches to drive out of London with unwanted babies, for dumping on the Common. Or he might have been a gypsy baby, or just the unwanted result of a local girl's mistake.

At all events, this particular foundling did not die, but was picked up by a farmer called Joseph Acres and taken home. He and his wife decided to adopt the little boy as a companion to their daughter. But what to call him? What name? What name? Soon they began calling him 'Whatname', and that in turn became Whatnay and finally Watney. And as for Daniel; well, wasn't he, like Daniel, delivered out of the lion's den? That, at least, is one legend.

Another, more frivolous, recounts that the baby had unusually large knees, and that when Mrs Acres first caught sight of the child, she exclaimed 'What knees!' The name stuck.

A few years ago, an American descendant of the family came up, after a great deal of patient research, with the suggestion that the original Watney was the descendant of a noble Flemish family called Whateau, or some such, who fled to England to escape persecution. This ingenious theory fails however to explain how the refugee found his way to Wimbledon Common.

A more mundane explanation sometimes put forward is that Daniel Watney was not a foundling at all, but was a farm labourer who lived at Sudbury, and for some reason removed himself to Wimbledon Common. In doing so, he invented a name for himself : perhaps using two names such as his father's and mother's, Watt and Ney. Or perhaps he was originally Wat (a fairly common Christian name) Ney. But if this is so, why should a foundling story ever have been put out at all?

On the whole, most of the family tend to accept the foundling story, if only, perhaps, because it is more romantic.

One fact however is absolutely certain, and that is that on 23 August, 1730, Daniel Watney, then aged twenty-five, married Mary Acres at St Mary's Church, Wimbledon.

Joseph Acres had no son of his own, and his daughter and son-in-law became his heirs. Daniel had three sons who survived childhood. The eldest, William, started brewing, but his main interest was still farming. The youngest brother, John Watney, became a member of the Mercers' Company, one of the oldest of the City Guilds, and eventually its Master. But though he made money in the City, he built up, with the help of his eldest son, a substantial business as a miller on the Wandle River, Wandsworth, a beautiful unspoilt piece of countryside.

It wasn't until the arrival of James Watney, John Watney's grandson, that the family became actively interested in brewing, outside the Wimbledon-Wandsworth area. In 1837 James, born in 1800, took a quarter share in the Stag Brewery in Pimlico.

It was a charming place, known as the 'Home Premises'. Wooded, with large open spaces, its main feature was Pimlico Lodge, described at the time as 'a capital family residence of handsome appearance with two wings and a colonnade'. This was where the original owners of the brewery, the Elliot family, lived.

The brewery itself was attached to one side of the house, but was approached by a separate entrance, so that the pleasure of the large property was not disturbed by the business except when the wind was in a certain direction, and the smell of malt wafted across the rose beds.

A farm was also situated within the property walls, where pigs, cows and chickens were bred. There was a pheasantry in the grounds, and stables, surmounted with a clock tower, cupola and belfry, capable of housing twenty horses. Mr Dingle, the brewer, lived in a house on the right of the Brewer Street entrance.

James Watney was a compulsive worker; while his wife was fanatically religious. Incredibly, despite her husband's occupation and the beer barrels that surrounded her, she was a staunch supporter of the teetotal movement. He compromised, by contributing from time to time large sums of money to the churches sponsored by his wife, and spent the rest of the time collecting one of the finest cellars of rare vintage port and old brandies, of the day.

The name of the firm changed from its original J. E. Elliot and Co., to Elliot Watney and Co., and was the ninth-largest brewery in London. The Elliot family and other partners sold out and soon James Watney, backed to the extent of £160,000 by his brother, was in sole control. By 1850, the firm had reached the eighth position.

In 1854, James Watney's son, also called James, became a partner in the firm at a fixed salary of £1,500 a year. James Watney I, as the father was soon called, held six-sevenths of the business, while James Watney II had to be content with one-seventh. In addition he had no security of tenure, his father being in complete control. So precarious was his position that once, when asked whether he was a partner of Elliot Watney and Co., he replied, 'I don't know if I shall be when I get back!'

In 1858, with the retirement of the last member of the Elliot family, the name of the firm was changed to James Watney and Co. The extent of the property had been reduced by two-thirds when Victoria Street was driven through it. All that part of 'Mr Elliot's Park' that used to stretch some distance down the Vauxhall Bridge Road was lost, or sold to the developers. With the building of Victoria Station on what used to be the Grosvenor Basin on the adjoining Duke of Westminster's estate, the whole character of the neighbourhood changed. Streets of small houses and shops sprang up; more plots of land were sold including one for the construction of the Victoria Palace Theatre; while the ever-expanding brewery, behind its closed walls, spread all over its restricted space, demolishing in its wake that residence 'of handsome appearance' Pimlico Lodge, its lawns and flower-beds, and all other traces of rural life.

During the next two decades James Watney and Co. rose steadily up the brewers' league table, until the company was at last the largest in London.

James Watney I lived to be eighty-four and retained control of the business almost to the end of his long life. He had moved from the original Watney environment of Wandsworth to Haling Park, Croydon, to be near his brother Daniel. There were, it was reported, seventy-two parsons in the district, enough to satisfy even his religious-minded wife.

When he died, his wife fulfilled a lifelong and secret ambition. She ordered the family butler to break off the necks of James Watney's precious old port and brandy bottles, and to pour the irreplaceable liquid down the sink. The family doctor, arriving by chance in the middle of this outrage, managed to save a few of the priceless bottles, by claiming them as medicine and having them all delivered to Guy's Hospital. It is not recorded whether this novel 'medicine' was for the benefit of the patients or the staff.

Mrs Watney continued to live for some time after her husband's death, but suffered severely from insomnia. Every morning, the butler came over to a nearby nephew's house with a bulletin of how the old lady fared. 'Mrs James's compliments,' he would say, 'and she didn't sleep well.' Later it might be : 'Mrs James's compliments and she had a better night.' One morning the butler arrived with the report : 'Mrs James's compliments and she died in the night.'

James Watney II was now in sole charge of the brewery. He was a Member of Parliament for the Eastern Division of Surrey; and in view of the fact that his two brothers had left the brewery some years earlier, and his two sons were not yet of age, he decided to turn the company into a limited liability company. The articles of association were drawn up, and a new company, Watney and Co. Ltd, came into being. It was valued at £2,060,000. Exhausted by the work and responsibility that had fallen upon him, particu-

larly since his father's death, James Watney lived only long enough
to see the new company launched, dying, at the age of fifty-four,
two years after his father.

The new company, like the old, prospered, but was no longer an
exclusive Watney concern. Outside directors were brought in. New
ones were added.

Among these were Charles Phillips and his brother Herbert,
who had been running the Mortlake Brewery on the Thames for
some years. Soon after the merger, a fire broke out at the brewery.
Mrs Walter Watney, who was later to marry Sir Edwin Lutyens's
brother, Francis, but who was then a young bride, always remem-
bered that fire.

'We were called out in the middle of the night,' she would say,
'and because there were no fire-engines, we made a human chain
down to the river; men, women and children passed the buckets
from hand to hand to the men who were fighting the fire. If we
hadn't put out the fire that night, there would have been no Mortlake Brewery today; for we were not insured.'

For some time the three large but separate breweries of Watney
and Co. Ltd, Combe and Co., and Reid's had been cautiously discussing the possibility of a merger, or as they preferred to put it, a
'get-together'. At last, after surmounting many problems, a new
company was born on 8 July, 1898. It was called Watney Combe
Reid and Co., and had a share issue of £15,000,000. Sir Cosmo
Bonsor of Combe's became chairman. Vernon Watney, James
Watney II's eldest son, became one of three deputy-chairmen,
while Claude Watney, Vernon's younger brother, became one of
nine other directors.

Thus, within a dozen years of the death of James Watney I, the
firm had more than trebled in size, but in doing so was no longer
the sole property of the Watney family.

The new company entered the new century confidently. The
Great War of 1914-18 had little effect on its affairs except to produce a shortage of man-power and transport. The post-war
Depression was surmounted, and once again another war had to be
faced. With the threat of invasion and Churchill's call for the for-
mation of Local Defence Volunteers, later to be called the Home
Guard, Watneys produced its own mobile transport unit. It consisted of a platoon of sixty men, six despatch riders and a fleet of

lorries with their slogans 'Reid's Stouts' and 'Watney's Ales' intact, in charge of thirty-six drivers.

Various properties, besides numerous public houses, were bombed. The Stag Brewery itself was hit several times. In April 1941, a delayed-action bomb blew up behind the stables; a month later the box-store was literally reduced to splinters by a bomb; more tragically, twelve of the company's twenty horses were killed when a bomb fell on the stables later that same night. The engineers' shop was also hit, scattering thousands of nuts and bolts. All were collected by the storemen in the morning.

One day, a report spread rapidly around the town that the main vats at the Stag Brewery had been hit, and that the streets around the premises were running with beer. Local inhabitants, it was said, were rushing out with every kind of container and scooping up the precious liquid. The baths in all the nearby Westminster houses were brimfull of 'buckshee' beer. Like so many rumours at the time, there appears to be little or no foundation of truth in this piece of wishful thinking.

Immediately after the war, much rebuilding had to be done, and there was the problem of the Stag Brewery itself. The London County Council wanted to drive a new road from Buckingham Palace Road to Victoria Street. At the same time, the planning authorities did not like the idea of keeping such a large industrial concern going so near Victoria Station. After considerable discussion, it was decided that the valuable site should be sold, enough land being kept to build a headquarters office, Watney House, for the firm. Mortlake could not be expanded sufficiently to cater for the demand created by the closing of the Stag Brewery, nor could any of the other breweries under the company's control. A solution was found in the merger with Mann, Crossman and Paulin Ltd.

On 23 April 1959, the last drop of beer was brewed at the Stag Brewery. The next day, for the first time in three hundred years, no beer was being brewed in Westminster, for the closing of the Stag Brewery marked the end of all brewing in the borough. At one time, there had been more breweries than private houses; now they were all gone.

Watney Mann Ltd, as the new company was called, was a much vaster, more complex affair than any of its predecessors. It branched out into other parts of the country, bringing the Watney red barrel to areas where it had never been seen before. It developed interests in other spheres. Inevitably it attracted the attention of the professional take-over experts. Charles Clore had already, in 1959, tried to take over the property side of the business, by making a bid for Watney Mann. He was not successful. But later, Maxwell Joseph of Grand Metropolitan Hotels succeeded in acquiring it.

Today, there are no members of the Watney family in the business. Of the last two Watneys, Oliver (Togo) Watney died recently, leaving £1,000,000 worth of paintings, including a number of Botticellis, at his Cornbury Park estate near Oxford; and Sanders Watney retired, although still retaining his interest in parading the Watney horses and driving the old 'Red Rover' London-Southampton stage-coach.

In all events, relatively few of the original descendants of Daniel Watney were involved with brewing. A number became distillers. One branch combined, through marriage, with the Gilbey gin family. One went to France and raced Bugattis at Le Mans, others became businessmen, stockbrokers, doctors and clergymen. One married into an old Danish family whose family tree went back to a Viking king who lived in 810, nine hundred years before the first Watney was found on Wimbledon Common.

But wherever they are or whatever they are doing, the tag 'a member of the famous brewing family' is sure to follow. It has its disadvantages: all Watneys are considered to be millionaires. Prospective employers are inclined to say : 'I'm afraid the salary we're offering is far too low for a Watney.' But it has its advantages. It is comforting to see one's name displayed in so many places. One could never, one feels, suffer from amnesia : there's always the 'Watney Wall' to help one find one's identity again.

Another famous brewing family are the Whitbreads. Samuel Whitbread, the founder of the business, was born at Cardington, near Bedford, on 30 August, 1720. Unlike young Daniel Watney, who was thirteen at the time, Samuel Whitbread came from well-recorded yeoman stock. There are references to the Wytbreads, or Blaunpaynes as they were sometimes called when using the Anglo-French equivalent (*blanc pain,* or *pain blanc* = white bread), as far back as the thirteenth century.

Samuel was the youngest of five sons in a family of eight children. In 1734, at the age of fourteen, his widowed mother, realizing that there would be no work for him as a farmer at home, sent him to London to be apprenticed to a brewer.

By 1742, he had learnt his trade sufficiently well to set himself up in business, with a partner called Shewell, in the neighbourhood of Golden Lane. In 1745 he acquired the Chiswell Street brewery next to a public house called the *Eagle and Child,* subsequently re-named the *King's Head.*

The joint business prospered. In 1760, when beer-tax was introduced, Whitbread's brewed 63,408 barrels of beer, an amount only to be surpassed in London by Calvert and Seward. It was in this year that the Porter Tun Room was constructed on the site of what had been four houses. Its great unsupported roof-span was exceeded in size only by that of Westminster Hall.

In 1761, Shewell retired, and Samuel Whitbread carried on the business alone. He had an enquiring earnest mind, and was of a very religious temperament. He combined a forward-looking liberal policy with philanthropic work; and, like many brewers, was concerned with the well-being of his employees.

In 1785, he engaged Smeaton, the engineer responsible for the Eddystone Lighthouse, to build a series of huge underground storage cisterns. Rennie, another famous engineer, adapted the brewery machinery to steam, and James Watt, of Boulton and Watt, built the Sun and Planet steam engine for the firm. When it was installed, this 'stupendous steam engine' was the wonder of London. In 1787, its fame was so great that George III and Queen Charlotte indicated that they would like to see the machine themselves. The visit was duly arranged. The *London Chronicle* had this to say of the auspicious occasion : 'The time appointed for the visit in Chiswell Street was ten in the morning on Saturday last. Curiosity and courtesy outran the clock. Their Majesties were there a quarter before ten. . . . They were received at the door by Mr Whitbread and his daughter; and politely declining the breakfast that was provided, immediately went over the works.'

The King, Queen, Princesses and courtiers were most impressed by everything they saw, the King taking trouble to explain the complicated machinery to the Queen, while the Princesses even squeezed through the door into the great cistern, where 4,000 barrels of beer were miraculously stored. As a result of this visit Smeaton's great underground vaults were named 'King's Vault' and 'Queen's Vault'.

A not so flattering account of the visit was written in satirical stanzas by Dr John Wolcot, under the pen-name of 'Peter Pindar'. It ran to 183 lines, and was published under the title *Instructions to a Celebrated Laureat alias Mr Whitbread's Brewery.*

> The monarch heard of Whitbread's fame;
>   Quoth he unto the queen, 'My dear, my dear,
> Whitbread hath got a marvellous great name,
>   Clearly, we must, must, must see Whitbread's brew.'

In the meantime Samuel Whitbread was getting his staff ready for the royal visit. His preparations are also satirized by 'Peter Pindar' :

> He gave his maids new aprons, gowns and smocks;
> And lo ! two hundred pounds were spent on frocks.

The King's extraordinarily minute interest in every detail of the brewery is recorded, as too is his habit of repeating words and questions in such a hurry that they sometimes came out as a mumble :

> And now his curious majesty did stoop
> To count the nails on every hoop;
> And lo ! no single thing came in his way,
> That full of deep research, he did not say,
> 'What's this? he, he? What's that? What's
> This? What's that?'
> So quick the words too when he deign'd to speak,
> As if each syllable would break its neck.

The King was so impressed by everything he saw that he began to take notes, even of the most insignificant matters. This curious trait of his pigeon-hole mind did not escape the satirist's attention :

> Now, majesty, alive to knowledge, took
> A very pretty memorandum-book,
> With gilded leaves of asses' skins so white,

And in it legibly did write –
    Memorandum,
A charming place beneath the grates,
For roasting chestnuts or potates.

Other non-sequiturs reputed to be recorded by the busy note-taking King are recounted by 'Peter Pindar', including the sensible and practical :

    Mem.
    Not to forget to take of beer the cask
    The brewer offered me, away.

Compared to many of the savage lampoons of the time, this was gentle, even complimentary. Samuel Whitbread, at least, had no cause for complaint. His brewery became even more well-known, its fame extending all over Europe.

Samuel Whitbread sat in Parliament as a member for Bedford, he gave large sums of money to charity, and had his portrait painted by Sir Joshua Reynolds. He died in 1796. But his 'stupendous steam engine' gave service for nearly another hundred years. When it finally retired, it emigrated to Australia, and found a home for itself in a museum in Sydney.

Samuel Whitbread's son, also called Samuel, was educated at Eton and Cambridge. He carried on the business alone for a few years after his father's death, but then set up a series of partnerships to deal with the day-to-day handling of affairs. His main interest was politics; he was a Member of Parliament from the time of his election in 1790 until his death in 1815, being known as 'Mr Whitbread, the Politician'. He married, at the age of twenty-four, the sister of one of his school friends, who was one day to become Earl Grey, and be responsible for steering the Reform Bill through Parliament. Although his father was not a Whig, father and son shared one common belief : the absolute need to abolish slavery. It was said that Samuel Whitbread I was the first man to call for the abolition of slavery. Meetings to enquire into the slave trade were held in his drawing room in Portman Square. Samuel Whitbread II carried on the crusade, and supported Wilberforce in his work.

By the end of the century, Whitbread's had become the largest brewers in London. In 1787, the output of Whitbread's brewery was 150,280 barrels; ten years later, it had risen to 192,747; by 1802, it was over 200,000 barrels. All of it was porter.

In 1809, Drury Lane Theatre was burnt down. Its owner, Richard Brinsley Sheridan, the dramatist and politician, watched it burn from a Covent Garden coffee-house, fortified with bumpers of port. When friends suggested that he should go to bed, he retorted : 'Surely a man might be allowed to take a glass of wine by his own fireside.'

Though ruined by the fire, the author of *The Rivals* and *The School for Scandal* would not allow himself to be down-hearted. His friends rallied round him. Samuel Whitbread II agreed to find subscribers and headed the committee in charge of rebuilding a new Drury Lane Theatre.

The new theatre was opened in 1812. A prize was offered for the best inaugural speech, but none came up to standard. A cartoon by George Cruikshank, published in 1814 and entitled 'The Theatrical Atlas', shows Edmund Kean as Richard III, carrying the new Drury Lane on his shoulders. The theatre is labelled 'Whitbread's Intire'. There is a portrait of Whitbread, dressed in a barrel, standing in the doorway of the theatre, saying 'Now, by St Paul, the work goes bravely on.'

Whitbread had hoped that the theatre would pay; but a passage in *The Farington Diary* of 1815 reads : 'He had induced several persons in Bedfordshire, his neighbours, to become subscribers to it, but it proved a disappointment, and with all He could do as manager of the concern He could not affect that a Dividend should be paid.'

He was one of the few people who got the better in repartee of Beau Brummell, the arbiter of fashion and a specialist in rudeness. When a small gambling debt was settled, Beau Brummell was heard to say, 'Thanks, mash tub, and in future I shall never drink any porter but yours.' To which Whitbread dryly replied : 'I only wish every other blackguard in London would do the same.'

Samuel Whitbread II died in 1815. His two sons, William Henry Whitbread and Samuel Charles Whitbread, entered into partnership in the business in 1819. Up till then Whitbread's had brewed only porter and stout, but after 1834 tastes began to change and they began to brew ale. This led to a great expansion of the business. A Speaker of the House of Commons married a daughter of Samuel Whitbread II, and as a result the brewery was granted permission to provide the horses for the Speaker's coach during official processions, such as coronations, jubilees and thanksgiving services.

The Whitbreads followed one upon the other, combining business and parliamentary careers. Indeed, from 1768 to 1910 there was always one member of the family, except for very brief intervals, sitting in Parliament. Louis Pasteur was among the many famous people who visited the brewery. He spent some time studying beer fermentations, the company providing him with special small fermenting vessels to help him. In 1899 the company became a limited liability company.

It survived many fires, thanks in large measure to the efficiency of its own brewery fire brigade. On one occasion, water being scarce, the fire-engine hoses were 'supplied from a large vat containing nearly 4,000 barrels of porter, in consequence of which the fire was soon extinguished'. It survived, almost alone in its bomb-devastated area, the 1940 and subsequent blitzes, and continues today with its work of supplying thirsty citizens with their well-earned refreshment. There are still members of the Whitbread family on the board.

Although Guinness is perhaps now the most famous name in brewing, it was not until well into the nineteenth century that it began to become well-known. Arthur Guinness had bought the lease of the original premises from Mark Rainsford in 1759, for 9,000 years, at a yearly rent of £45. It had only one mash tun and one seventy-barrel copper. Even in 1809, Guinness was only the second-largest brewery in Ireland, coming after Beamish and Crawford of Cork, who brewed 100,000 barrels a year.

The brewery concentrated on the production of porter, and by the middle of the nineteenth century this porter had become so popular that it was even able to compete with the English brews in London itself.

Contrary to popular belief, the dark black liquid, so distinctive of Guinness, does not use the waters of the Liffey in Dublin, dark though they may appear at times; but, more prosaically, those of the city watercourses. Guinness is now made in many places outside

Dublin.

The Guinness family retained close control of the business. When the original Arthur Guinness died in 1803 at the age of seventy-eight, the brewery was run by his second, fourth and fifth sons; on their deaths, the whole operation became the responsibility of Benjamin Lee Guinness, Arthur Guinness's grandson. It was Benjamin Guinness's sons, Arthur and Edward, who took the titles of Lord Ardilaun and Lord Iveagh respectively. In 1886, the business was turned into a limited liability company, and sold to the public for £6,000,000, the family retaining the chairmanship and other important positions.

A curious fact is that the popularity of Guinness grew almost entirely without publicity. It was already an established household name when the famous Guinness animals and the 'Guinness for Strength' advertisements appeared.

Its appeal rested on its medicinal qualities. Mention has already been made of its use during the Second World War as a cordial for convalescent soldiers. This battle use of Guinness goes back, however, to the Napoleonic Wars. A cavalry officer, wounded at Waterloo, wrote that : 'When I was sufficiently recovered to take some nourishment, I felt the most extraordinary desire for a glass of Guinness, which I knew could be obtained without difficulty. Upon expressing my wish to the doctor, he told me I might take a small glass. . . . I thought I had never tasted anything so delightful. . . . I am confident that it contributed more than anything else to the renewal of my strength.'

It was used again in great quantities during the 1914-18 War. Unsolicited testimonies poured in from doctors working in the various battlefields. One doctor wrote : 'We found Guinness the most valuable of all the "medical comforts" in my field ambulance in France 1917.' Others praised it as an antidote to influenza, insomnia, dysentery, sand-fly fever and malaria.

In fact, Guinness was more than just 'good for you'. It was a life-saver.

'Take Courage' is a pun in the true brewing tradition, exhorting one to be fearless and to drink the products of one of the greatest of brewing families. The first Courage to enter the brewing business was John Courage. He was the younger son of a French Huguenot family that had settled in Aberdeen in the middle of the seventeenth century. John himself had built up, by 1787, a successful maritime trade. His ships operated from Glasgow Wharf, near the Tower of London.

Across the river, on the south bank, was an open piece of land called Horselydown where fairs had flourished in the sixteenth century. Here for centuries ale had been brewed, until the name Southwark Ales had become famous throughout the land.

John Courage's initial investment was modest enough. A cheque dated 20 December, 1787 for £616 13s 11d gave him control of the Anchor Brewhouse, Horselydown. In the first year of business, the brewery turned out 51 barrels of beer.

But in the years that followed, he built up the brewing side of his interests to such an extent that at his death in 1793, it was as a brewer rather than a shipper that he was known.

His widow, Harriet, then managed the business with the help of John Donaldson, the managing clerk, until she died in 1797. The only son in the family, also named John, was seven years old. Donaldson carried on the business until John Courage II was fourteen, when he joined the firm at the not unreasonable salary of £60 a year.

John Courage II and John Donaldson carried on together until Donaldson retired in 1836. The business prospered so much that it was now valued at £151,215.

John Courage II lived until 1854. In the fifty years that he worked at the brewery he built it up into one of the finest in London and consolidated his family's position in it. In 1837, he took his two older sons, John and Robert, into the business. After that the family's control of the business was absolute.

But in May 1891, disaster struck. Brewhouses have always been subject to fire-hazard. In May of that year, there was an explosion in the malt mills, and this set fire to the inflammable malt dust. The brewhouse burnt violently for days on end. Even the celebrated Captain Shaw with his new fire-engines and water-floats with their powerful jets could not save the place. It was a total loss.

And yet, within four weeks, beer was once again being brewed at Horselydown. By 1897, the yearly output had reached 333,400 barrels. It survived the 1914-18 War and the family's holding had, if possible, increased even more. There were no less than seven Courages working in the business at that time.

The 1939-45 War brought considerable damage to the brewhouse, for it was situated in one of the main target areas of the German bombers. The roof of the brewhouse was blown off completely, and the wall along the river side knocked down. But the buildings were in any case due for reconstruction, and in 1954 new buildings were put up and Courage's continued to prosper.

It was, literally, but a stone's throw from John Courage I's small brewhouse to Barclay, Perkins and Co.'s large establishment. Robert Barclay and John Perkins, with two other partners, David Barclay and Silvanus Bevan, had, as we have already seen, bought Thrale's Brewery at Southwark after the latter's death in 1781.

Perkins had been chief clerk under Thrale's direction, and indeed had ambitions to become a partner even while Thrale was alive, a fact that shocked Mrs Thrale considerably. 'Perkins,' she wrote once, 'takes every step to worm himself into this proposed partnership.'

Robert Barclay, on the other hand, was a brother of David Barclay, who was a partner in Barclays Bank. One day when David was out walking with his fellow director, Silvanus Bevan, they saw the notices of the sale of Thrale's Brewery.

'This business will do for young Robert,' said David.

And, indeed, within three months, the deal was completed. It took four years for Perkins to find his share of the money; but he had got what he wanted : a partnership in the firm, and, in addition, Thrale's old house at the brewery itself.

The new firm flourished. By 1802, Barclay Perkins had pushed up their 1781 sales of 80,053 barrels to 137,405, second only to Meux. Seven years later, by 1809, they had overtaken Meux, with an output of 205,328 barrels.

They too, just like Courage's at a later date, were devastated by fire. It occurred in 1832. Another Barclay, Charles, who was busy across the river in Parliament was told about the fire. He immediately left the House and took charge of the fire-fighting equipment. Damage worth £40,000 was done, but thanks to the fire-fighters saving much of the stock of beer and the fact that another Barclay Perkins brewery in Stoney Lane was unaffected, customers were kept in full supply.

After its rebuilding, the brewery became a famous attraction for foreign visitors. Some were not always welcome. It is recorded that when a certain Baron von Haynau, known as the 'Hyena of Brescia' because of the brutal way he had suppressed a rebellion in Italy, visited Barclay Perkins' brewery in 1850, he was greeted with cries of 'Down with the Austrian butcher!' Somebody dropped a truss of hay on his head, and the brewery draymen yelled and hissed at him. Many of the women from Southwark, incensed at the stories of his cruelties, particularly to women, joined the draymen in pursuit of the baron. He managed to escape from the crowd, and ran, terror-stricken, along Bankside. Finally, he reached the *George* public house, where he hid for a while in a dustbin, his pursuers beating about the tortuous passageways of the inn. He was eventually rescued by a police launch, which rowed him to safety across the river. Though he escaped with his life, he seemed to have lost his enormous Austrian moustaches, whether pulled out by the infuriated populace or prudently cut off to disguise himself, is not revealed.

The incident caused considerable international turmoil. Palmerston, much against his inclinations, had to apologize formally to the Austrian government, but did so in a way to show that he sympathized with the Barclay Perkins draymen. Public opinion was strongly on the side of the brewers. Ballads in praise of the draymen were composed. Their 'noble conduct' was officially approved at a public meeting at Farringdon Hall in September of that year.

Echoes of the incident continued for years. Because of the 'slight' to von Haynau, the Austrians refused to send a representative to the Duke of Wellington's funeral in 1852. Later still, when Garibaldi, the great liberator of Italy, visited London in 1864, he insisted on visiting the brewery where English 'freedom lovers' had struck the first blow against the 'tyrant' von Haynau.

Although Courage and Barclay Perkins were, for many years, rivals, it was Barclay Perkins who came to Courage's assistance at the time of Courage's great fire in 1891. Barclay Perkins supplied all the beer Courage needed while Courage's own brewhouse was out of action.

In 1896, Barclay Perkins, still with members of the original families in control, became a public company. After the 1914-18 War, the firm launched Barclay's Lager; it had a great and immediate success both at home and abroad. It expanded by taking over Style and Winch Ltd and other breweries in 1929.

For some time tentative negotiations had been going on between Courage and Barclay Perkins. In 1955, the two companies merged, and for the first time members of all the original families concerned sat together as directors of the same brewery.

Of all the great brewing names, Truman must surely hold the record for being the longest in the business. There was a William Truman at work on his tubs as far back as 1381. His entry into recorded history was not, however, on account of the excellence, or otherwise, of the ale he brewed, but because, in a moment of political excitement, during the Wat Tyler rebellion, he struck the Lord Mayor of London.

Nothing more was heard of the Trumans until 1613, when the Middlesex Sessions Rolls recorded the existence in the parish of St Giles Without Cripplegate of another William Truman, also registered as a brewer.

It was not, however, until Joseph Truman set up business in 1666 that the firm really came into being. He acquired a brewery in Brick Lane. By the end of the century he had done well and had acquired sufficient respectability to be elected a churchwarden in 1699. He was succeeded by his two sons, Joseph, who retired fairly soon, and Benjamin, who made the name nationally famous. He was helped in this by a curious incident. In 1737, the Prince of Wales ordered a huge celebratory bonfire to be burnt in front of Carlton House. Four barrels of beer were provided by the Royal Brewer to slake the thirst of those who partook in the celebrations. The beer, however, was of inferior quality. There was an immediate riot, the indignant 'guests' throwing the barrels into the bonfire. The Prince of Wales, sensibly enough, ordered another bonfire to be lit the following evening. This time he asked Benjamin Truman to provide the beer. He sent along his very finest beer, 'with which,' as the record puts it, 'the populace was pleased and satisfied.'

When George III came to the throne in 1760, Benjamin Truman was knighted. The firm had turned by then to the production of porter; and, with an output of 60,140 barrels, was the third largest brewer in London.

Benjamin Truman died on 16 March, 1780, in his eighty-first year. His only son had died long before him, in 1766, leaving no direct heir to the business. However, he provided for the children of his granddaughter, Frances, to come into the business eventually.

In the meantime, as in so many other cases, the head clerk, in this case James Grant, took over the running of the business. When he himself died in 1789, his share was sold to a young man called Sampson Hanbury, who was to run the brewery single-handed for the next forty-six years, Truman's great-grandsons preferring to remain sleeping partners and collecting their revenues, rather than working at the brewery itself.

As time went on, two other families, the Buxtons and the Pryors, joined the firm. Soon the name Truman Hanbury Buxton became a synonym for good beer, an enlightened employer-employee relationship and a certain position in the world of literature. Charles Dickens, for example, had Mrs Micawber say, with sublime if ill-judged optimism, of her mercurial husband, that he was 'particularly adapted to the brewing business – look at Truman Hanbury and Buxton'. A number of Truman public houses were featured in *Pickwick Papers.*

Like Whitbread's, Truman's attracted the interest of people of high position. On one occasion in 1831, the Prime Minister, Lord Chancellor and a number of other distinguished guests sat down to a dinner of steaks and porter at the brewery in Spitalfields. Before dinner, the great new steam engine that had recently been installed was inspected, the Lord Chancellor holding forth at considerable length on its merit. After dinner, the party visited the stables where the garrulous Lord Chancellor, perhaps under the influence of the porter, wanted to ride a horse.

In 1873, Truman's bought Phillips' Brewery at Burton-on-Trent, so that the famous beer of that town could be available to Truman customers. In 1889, the company became public. Through it all, the ghost of old Sir Benjamin Truman presided over the company; for, after him, there were no Trumans brewing actively. So powerful had been his influence that his name continued. Even now, when Truman's is a part of Grand Metropolitan, the old man's name goes marching on.

If any one family can be said to have 'owned' the British Army at any time, it must surely be Simonds.

The connection was initially a matter of chance. William Blackall Simonds came from a prosperous Berkshire family, which had been active in the area since Saxon days. Simonds himself was a

banker in Reading as well as a brewer. He began brewing in 1785
in Broad Street, Reading, before moving his expanding business
to the west bank of the Kennet. It was a strategic move, for barges
up to 110 tons in weight could travel as far as Newbury and, via
the Kennet and Avon Canal, could reach Bath and Bristol. More
important still was a provision in his father's will, dated 1765,
which gave him 'all my Farm and Land in the Parish of Sandhurst'. When the Royal Military College opened there in 1813,
Simonds was on the spot. By June 1814 he was supplying beer to
the college. It is said that when news of Waterloo was received,
the victory was duly toasted at Sandhurst with Simonds' beer.

Simonds' successors, who were also members of the same family,
concentrated on the army connection. In 1853 Aldershot was
bought as a training area and after the Crimean War it was turned
into a permanent camp. Manoeuvres for both the regular and
militia forces became more and more complex. Simonds' developed a highly successful 'intelligence service' which always let the
firm know, long before anyone else, the date and location of
scheduled manoeuvres. This meant that the brewery could have
all its barrels and bottles out on the site even before the troops
arrived. In fact, so good was this unofficial intelligence service that
when commanding officers wanted to know when and where their
unit was due to go on manoeuvres, they would consult the
'Simonds' man' because he would be sure to know.

The firm produced its own tents and field equipment, so that it
would not be at all unusual for a battalion to arrive at its allocated
training area to find Simonds' tents, with flags flying, already in
position, the barrels tapped and the Simonds' assistants ready to
pour out the welcome liquid.

In 1898, so colossal was the Army's deployment that Simonds'
not only used all their own horses, but hired every available horse
in Reading to keep their tents stocked with beer. In the huge 1911
manoeuvres they used motor transport for the first time.

In Victorian times, wherever the British Army went, Simonds'
beer was sure to go: South Africa, Gibraltar, Malta, Egypt,
Sudan, the Middle East and the Far East. Even after the NAAFI
(Navy, Army and Air Force Institutes) was formed, Simonds' connection with the Army continued, and the partnership still
flourishes today.

The brewing of beer in Scotland was for many years hampered by the Act of Union of 1706, in which the government imposed a tax on malt. On 28 August, 1725, the brewers of Edinburgh decided not to brew any more beer in protest against the taxes. The striking brewers were fined and some were even imprisoned, and although the strike had collapsed by 2 September, the resentment against beer taxes continued for many years. Many Scotsmen switched from drinking beer to their own native drink, whisky. To this day whisky is still the more popular of the two drinks.

Nevertheless some brewers did make a success out of beer brewing. Among the most prominent was William Younger, who set up a brewery at Leigh, where the waters were particularly pure, in 1749. In 1778, a relation of his, Archibald C. Younger, founded his own brewery at Edinburgh. The beer he brewed was so powerful that, according to contemporary testimony, it 'almost glued the lips together'. The two family concerns were amalgamated under another William Younger in 1821.

Scottish nomenclature is rather different to the English. Bitter is known as 'heavy beer'; mild is rarely found. On the whole, Youngers' ales and stouts, including the almost legendary 'Newcastle Brown', are stronger than their equivalents south of the border. They have to be, to compete with whisky!

Many other breweries have sprung up, merged and prospered throughout the land. There's Strong, whose advertisements proclaimed, as the traveller went west, that he was entering the Strong Country, George's of Bristol, Smith's of Tadcaster, Young's and Ind Coope of London, and Meux whose 22-foot-high vat in the Tottenham Court Road burst its hoops in 1814. In the subsequent flood of porter eight people died, some drowned by the beer, some buried in the houses demolished by the flood, and one from sheer drunkenness from this unexpected bonanza.

There was Barnstable ale, Yorkshire ale, Derbyshire ale, Banbury ale and many others large and small, which could echo the song in praise of Burton ale :

> Ne'er tell me of liquors from Spain or from France,
> They may get in your heels and inspire you to dance,
> But Ale of old Burton if mellow and right
> Will get in your head and inspire you to fight.

Then Molly approach with your Peacock and Cann –
Not Juno herself brought more blessings to man –
With nip after nip, all my sorrows beguile,
And my Fortune and Mistress shall presently smile.

Nor is the special family relationship so often found in the production of beer, special to one country alone. The founding of the
great Danish firm of Carlsberg is a family story.

Christen Jacobsen left his parents' farm in Jutland towards
the end of the eighteenth century and set himself up as a brewer in
Copenhagen. He was the first Danish brewer to use a thermometer
instead of merely putting his hand into the beer to test its temperature. His son, Jacob Christian Jacobsen, born in 1811, was brought
up in Brolæggerstræde, the street where the brewery was situated.
After his father's death in 1835, he took over the business.

In 1845 he went to Munich, bringing back two quarts of real
Bavarian yeast. At every single stop on the long stage-coach
journey back to Copenhagen, he would get out, and fill the containers with fresh water in order to keep the yeast alive. As soon as
he got back, he started brewing real Bavarian or 'Lager' beer as
it was called. He bought some land in the Copenhagen suburb of
Valby, close to where the first Danish railway was being built, and
put up a brewery which he called Carlsberg, in honour of his
young son, Carl.

J. C. Jacobsen, or 'the captain' as he was known after his service
in the Civic Guard, built up a huge business, endowed the arts and
constructed a large house for himself. His son, the very same Carl
after whom the first brewery and lager was called, was as enterprising as his father. He branched out on his own and built up a
huge new brewery called Ny Carlsberg (New Carlsberg). Like his
father, who died in Rome in 1887, Carl Jacobsen was also a great
benefactor and keen patron of the arts. The Ny Carlsberg brewery
is probably the only one in the world deliberately designed to look
like a civic building, while performing a commercial purpose. He
filled Copenhagen with statues, including the world-famous Little
Mermaid, sitting on her rock on Langelinie, overlooking the har-
bour. He founded the Ny Carlsberg Glyptothek, and stocked it
with paintings, sculptures and archaeological objects, until it
became one of the world's greatest museums.

In 1906, he amalgamated his various interests and formed the Carlsberg Breweries. He became its first manager, and remained as such until his death in 1914.

Today, the Carlsberg Breweries are the property of the state and are run as a huge world-wide concern; but the spirit of the original Jacobsen family remains, and can be seen in the close interest this international brewery still takes in the promotion of the arts.

Chapter Fifteen

The old methods of personal advertising we examined earlier soon gave way to the techniques of mass advertising. Beer, as a commodity, began in the 1930s to be advertised for its own sake, rather than for a particular brewery or brand. Under the guidance of the Brewers' Society, the successor to the old Brewers' Company, beer itself was popularized.

It was at this stage that Mr XXX first made his appearance. He consisted of a tankard of beer, conventionally drawn with handle and froth complete. In the beer itself, as if pickled, was a jolly, smiling, male face. Two line-drawing legs and arms completed the picture. He was accompanied by a 'talk-balloon' that conveyed a simple message such as 'Beer is Best'.

The slogans of the 'thirties were usually of this admonitory and healthy type. It was the heyday of the boy scout and the hiker. Already the generations were subconsciously getting ready for the coming war. 'Our forefathers thrived on British beer; *so can you*' went one slogan. Nor was the patriotic note forgotten : 'When you buy beer, you benefit yourself, the British farmer and the British Exchequer.'

Only somewhat grudging reference was made to the weaker members of society, and even this was of a hearty 'get-well-soon' type. Beer 'set a man up for winter'; it brought 'sunny warmth on sunny days'; it 'rounded off a square meal'. Even the jingles and doggerel verses that often accompanied the advertisements had the same slant.

One, specifically addressed to the hikers who tramped about the 1930s countryside, ran :

Beneath our feet the roads wind by,

126

> The pleasant fields unfold;
> The larks are singing in the sky
> Of cloudless blue and gold,
> And though our thirst's incredible,
> An inn will soon appear,
> Then won't our cup indeed be full –
> And full of what? Of beer!

Bert Thomas was commissioned to produce a series of drawings – usually simple, free-flowing sketches with a straightforward 'Beer is Best' message. One showed a schoolmaster spanking a boy and pointing to a blackboard where the famous slogan is inscribed. Another depicted a motorist, lost in a fog, climbing a sign post. In the light of his torch can again be made out the words: 'Beer is Best.'

Mr XXX, like many characters connected with beer, was a great one for puns. He would announce himself as 'His Xcellency the Minister of the Inn-terior', and would address his readers as 'Friends, Yeomen and Countrymen'. He was, he declared, 'a son of the soil and as British as the weather,' adding in something of an non sequitur, 'that is why no other drink is better for you than British beer.'

He liked to 'Xpound', as he called it, on a variety of subjects and was full of information. Did we know, he demanded, that the Devil was afraid to cross the Tamar into Cornwall because the women would turn him into a pastie?

He had a wife, Mrs XXX, who was somewhat under his domination, and spent most of her time making Yorkshire Pudding, Lancashire Hot Pot, Norfolk Herring Pie and other dishes.

Not all the advertisements were of this simple punning or homely type. As war approached the government encouraged its potential fighters, both men and women, to get out into the country and to become as fit as possible. It had been alarmed by the statistics of sub-growth, particularly in the densely-populated urban areas. Many children grew up to adulthood without ever having seen the country. Even children who had parks near the home knew nothing of the countryside. Taken there, and seeing such acres of pastureland, they would ask, in awe, 'Can we walk on the grass?'

Commerce followed the lead given by the government. The Brewers' Society, along with other bodies of the same type, launched series of advertisements depicting life in the country. In 1938, a series entitled *A Calendar of British Beer* depicted a rural scene only indirectly related to beer itself. The one for October 1938 – immediately after Munich – showed a peaceful threshing scene, complete with belching steam engine, thresher and busy farm workers. Presumably the grain was barley. Another showed a hop field in preparation. Indirect advertising, then a novelty, was being tried out in many industries. The series was extremely popular.

As war grew nearer, however, the boisterous Mr XXX returned. He was now armed with a banner with the words 'For a fitter Britain' printed across it. He seemed somehow to be a more serious-looking person than the jovial extrovert who could tell you, without a blink, the difference between a pastie and a hoggan (it's something to do with the way the pastry is sealed). He had a friend too, whom he introduced as the P.T. Instructor. The letters P.T. stood for 'Pint Tankard', not 'Physical Training'. But he used the standard instructor's jargon : 'On the word of command – ONE – take the vessel at the point of balance between the thumb and fingers of the right hand – TWO – bring the vessel smartly to the lips – THREE – cant the vessel slowly backwards, giving fair play to the force of gravity.'

When the war itself started, the tone of the advertisements became more positive and patriotic. The spirit of the 1914-18 War was evoked in bringing back the famous songs of that war : 'Pack Up Your Troubles in Your Old Kit Bag', 'Keep the Home Fires Burning', and 'If You Were the Only Girl in the World.' The early songs of the 1939-45 War did not come up to the same standard, perhaps because during the Phoney War period of 1939 it did not seem like war at all. The black-out, the restrictions on travel and the closing of many cinemas seemed more important than the war itself. When the Nazis overran Europe and only Britain and the Commonwealth were left in the war there seemed nothing to sing about. It was to be a German song 'Lili Marlene' that was to epitomize this war as 'It's a Long Way to Tipperary' and others like it summed up the previous one.

One song, however, did catch on : 'Roll Out the Barrel'. It was

11 A fermenting room at Tetley's Warrington brewery.

10 A hop cold store at a modern brewery.

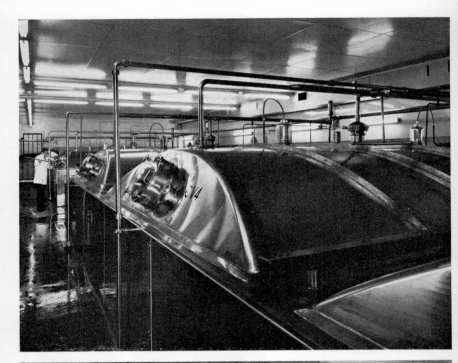

12   Gauging vessels for Harp lager.

13   The control room of a modern brewery.

said to have been inspired by the discovery, and liking, of English beer by Canadian soldiers arriving in ever-increasing numbers.

Presently, however, all advertising stopped. The Society handed over all its advertising space to the Ministry of Information. A long series of 'What do I do?' advertisements then appeared. They had nothing to do with beer but answered questions to do with daily life in war-time. Some of them were vital: 'What do I do if I hear news that Germans are trying to land or have landed?'; 'What do I do if my home is made uninhabitable by a bomb?' and 'What do I do to keep my Anderson Shelter healthy in winter?' Some, however, were frankly surrealist: 'What do I do to improve my bone salvage?' 'What do I do to make my old rags fight?' What indeed?

Punch had a drawing in 1940 satirizing these messages and at the same time showing how popular they were: a sentry is challenging a citizen with the words: 'Halt, who goes there?' The citizen replies: 'Half a minute while I look up "What do I do?"''

Even when the war ended, the admonitory type of announcement continued. This time notices explained the need for restrictions on brewing. The slogan was: 'What – No beer?'

There were references to the feelings of soldiers still abroad or not yet demobilized. Browning's 'Home-thoughts from Abroad' was somewhat adapted, and read:

> It's oh, to be in England now,
> To walk an English lane,
> To see an English girl – and drink,
> Good English beer again.

Slowly however, the men returned and were demobilized. The Americans and Canadians left, taking with them, as the Agent General for Ontario noted, happy memories of the intimacy and friendliness of the pub, an institution that they did not have in their own countries.

Advertising space was restored to the Brewers' Society and direct advertising could begin once again. But there was still an echo of indirect advertising. Between December 1946 and April 1947, Mervyn Peake was commissioned to produce a series of illustrations of country scenes. These included a number of games such as darts, cricket, bowls, dominoes and shove-ha'penny. They touched on inns, fishing, hunting, gossip and friendship. There was a particularly attractive one about pigeon racing. Unlike the rest of the advertisements they all carried a line 'Specially illustrated by Mervyn Peake.' The originals have vanished. Perhaps they are in some collector's file? Reproductions, however, can still be seen at the Brewers' Society headquarters in Portman Square.

Peake's work for the Society did not continue for long. A dispute arose about the placing of a tree in one of the drawings. The Society pointed out that if it were left in its present position it would undermine an inn, shown behind it, and bring it down. Would Peake kindly move the inn back? Peake wrote from Sark, where he was then living, pointing out that if he did this, the all-important composition of the drawing would be destroyed. Artistic felicity was more important than architectural exactitude. The Society however was adamant. The inn or the tree, or both, must be removed. Although in need of the money, Peake could not compromise on a matter of principle and resigned. This was his only venture into the world of commercial art.

The Society continued to advertise graphically for some years; but with the advent of television, stopped all newspaper advertisements and turned instead to the new medium.

Today the Brewers' Society has ceased all forms of advertisement. Costs have become too high. Advertising for beer, whether in the press or on television has become once again the sole responsibility of individual breweries. Whether because of the popularity of the product or the skill of the practitioners in advertising, beer advertisements often seem to capture the imagination of the public more readily than those for other products. Slogans like 'Guinness Is Good For You' and 'What We Want Is Watneys' were known to all sections of society, chiefly from the imaginative posters that were so numerous. Today's television advertisements, explaining so succinctly 'what your right arm's for', seem to enjoy an equal popularity.

Chapter Sixteen

There is no record of how much the Ancient Egyptians charged for *hek,* or whether brewing was profitable then; but there is a general belief that anybody connected with beer must be well-off.

After all, goes the argument, people drink when they are happy, and they drink when they are sad. They drink when business is booming; they drink in times of depression. They drink to celebrate; they drink to mourn. Often they drink simply because they are thirsty or because they think it is good for them. Or because they feel sociable. So all this must be profitable.

It was certainly not the case in early British history. The Danish thanes who brought the drink here got their supplies from unpaid servants. The monasteries brewed their own supplies. The lords ordered a certain number of their serfs to grow the barley, to make the malt, brew and distribute.

Even in the little hamlets that made up the pattern of medieval Britain, the brewer was a modest member of the community. His cottage was one of the smallest and furthest away from the village centre. He worked on his own. His wife and sometimes his children helped him. He would spend much of the year tilling and hoeing, sowing the barley and then bringing it in. If he could not grow it himself he would have to go out and bargain for it. It was his wife who usually made the malt, while he would do the heavy work. His sons would help him to distribute the ale. By the end of the year, there was not very much profit to show.

During the greater part of the Middle Ages the price of ale was fixed by law, and remained constant. Only two kinds of ale were allowed to be brewed: the better and the second, called double and single. In Henry III's reign (1216-1272), the better kind of ale was fixed at one penny for two gallons if sold in a city, and one

penny for four gallons in the country. It obviously paid to live in
the country.

Nearly a hundred years later, in Edward III's reign (1327-
1377), the position had not altered very much. A new third ale had
been added. It was known as best ale, and cost as much as a penny
ha'penny a gallon. And three hundred years after that, in the early
part of Henry VIII's reign, the price of best ale was still exactly the
same. The Brewers' Company had been trying for many years to
raise the price, but it was not until 1533 that they finally managed
to get a moderate rise in price of both the 'doble' and the 'syngall'.

But even that was not enough to make their business lucrative;
so they resorted to cunning and started brewing what they called
'doble-doble' beer. It was admittedly very strong, but it meant that
they could charge double for it. They soon ceased to produce single
beer at all, but concentrated on the double-double beer – a practice
that enraged Henry's beer-loving daughter Elizabeth when she
came to the throne. With her usual briskness, Elizabeth issued a
Royal Proclamation ordering every brewer to brew 'as much
syngall as doble beare and more'. But the brewers seem, for once,
to have ignored the Queen's orders; for three years later, the irate
Queen, incensed at what she called their 'ungodly gredyness',
abolished double-double beer altogether. The brewers were forced
back to producing double and single only.

The government's attempts to impose fixed prices on the brewers
continued until the middle of the seventeenth century. By then
three sorts of beer were allowed : the best at eight shillings a barrel,
the second at six shillings and the small at four shillings. After that
price-fixing by the government was abolished. Beer prices were
allowed to find their own level on the market. The day of the big
fortunes was at hand.

But if the government ceased to control the price of beer, they
came up with a new idea : taxation. Although Charles I had taxed
beer in 1643, it was Charles II who, forever seeking new ways to
raise funds, fully established the practice. He charged a stiff one
shilling and threepence on beer selling at more than six shillings
per barrel, and threepence on small beer, which sold at under six
shillings per barrel.

These beer taxes were intended to apply for three years only,
but just as, at a later date, D.O.R.A. outlived her expected time, so

the beer taxes continued to be renewed; and at each renewal they were raised a bit more.

In order to assess exactly the amount of tax to be paid on any barrel, the excisemen marked the barrels with a cross. A single X denoted a weak brew and carried the minimum tax. A double XX was stronger and more highly taxed. The excisemen were in fact using symbols that had been in existence since medieval days, when much of the ale brewed came from monasteries. The X's were the sign of the Cross and showed that the monks had 'blessed' the barrels in question. The more blessings, the stronger the brew. These crosses were thus an early form of trademark. The custom was continued by the coopers, who marked their barrels in this way, and was finally taken over by the taxman.

Although the tax itself was abolished in the middle of the nineteenth century, the habit of marking barrels with crosses to denote the beer's strength continues to this day.

As well as beers of different strengths there were also special beers such as 'stoutt', the name originally given to an extra-strong, almost liqueur type of drink, that was decanted and drunk in fluted, port-style glasses. Eventually losing its after-dinner appeal, a similar drink called stout was produced that could be drunk at any time. Despite its name, it was supposed to be much favoured by ladies to keep the female form in good shape.

Another special and extremely popular type of beer was porter. This was not a special brew but a mixture of different types of ale and beer. Its name is said to derive from the fact that it was the favourite drink of the porters and marketmen who needed a good early-morning drink to give them strength. A form of porter was made in Ireland, called Irish porter. This, in turn, led to Guinness, which is like the original London porter but more bitter. Porter continued to be the most popular of mixed drinks for over a century. Only Guinness has maintained the popularity once held by porter.

Although porter was the most appreciated of mixtures there have been many others. Publicans and innkeepers will often experiment with mixtures. Mild and bitter, a mixture of mild ale and strong beer, was much in demand during and just after the Second World War. It is still fairly popular, but more exotic mixtures such as bitter and lime have tended to take its place.

The early alehouse brewing equipment was very simple. All that was needed was a copper, a fermenting vessel and some casks. But as the business developed so the equipment became more complex and expensive. Sometimes brewers would band together and share their customers among each other. They were known as common brewers. By the middle of the sixteenth century there were twenty-six common brewers in the City of London and the immediate surrounds. Twenty were on the south bank of the Thames, six on the north. Between them, they produced 650,000 barrels a year.

They were the first of the wealthy brewers; and they began the tradition of giving part of their profits to charity and to the foundation of schools.

The number of brewers continued to increase. A hundred years later the original twenty-six brewers in London had increased to 199. There were a further 675 in the rest of England and Wales.

Though Dr Johnson's estimates of the fortunes to be obtained from brewing may have been optimistic, this was the time when the big breweries began to expand and centres outside London started to take on a new importance to the trade.

One of these was Burton-on-Trent. Ale had been brewed there for centuries. There are records of monastic, though not of public, brewing in the neighbourhood of the town as far back as the thirteenth century. By the sixteenth century, Burton had achieved a local fame. When that much-travelled and beer-loving lady, Queen Elizabeth I, proposed to visit Tutbury Castle, she made Walsingham, who was in charge of the preparations for the journey, write to Sir Ralph Sadler, Governor of Tutbury Castle, and ask : 'What place neere Tutbury beere may be provided for her Majestie's use?' Sir Ralph replied : 'At Burton three myles off.'

By the middle of the next century Burton ale was being sold in London in direct competition with the local brews. The *Peacock* in Gray's Inn Lane became famous as a rendezvous for lovers of Burton ale. The excellence of this ale was due to the purity of the spring waters at Burton. Just as in the Thames, these were unusually clear. In addition, they had the special purity that meant that when saccharine was mixed with the water it retained its strength and quality almost indefinitely. Burton ale remained fresh and delectable long after many other brews had gone flat.

The opening of the Trent Navigation and other canals at the

beginning of the eighteenth century confirmed Burton-on-Trent's fame as a brewing centre. It was cheaper and easier to convey the barrels down to London or across country to the ports serving Northern Europe and Russia. Soon not only had the home trade expanded enormously but a flourishing export trade was established. Russia was a particularly good customer. Peter the Great and the Empress Catherine loved Burton ale. So much so that special Russian ales were brewed. The name 'Russian' can still be found on certain brews.

The trade with Russia was carried through Hull as well as London. A barter agreement existed whereby Russian goods were exchanged at St Petersburg for Burton ale. These goods were then imported and sold for considerably more than the cost of making and exporting the ale.

It was commonplace to use the sea and canals for transporting goods from one part of the country to another. Roads were few and those that did exist were in appalling condition, main roads being often little more than rutted lanes. Wagons drawn by shire horses were slow, and the cost of road transport was enormous. There were no railways.

The open sea, and the long, smooth canals provided an ideal and cheap method of transporting heavy loads. While small vessels moved down the coast from port to port, long, narrow barges sailed silently down the canals. It was, and still is (though now with some difficulty), possible to sail all the way from London to Hull entirely by canal. Customers, when ordering their Burton ales, would specify whether the goods were to be sent by sea or canal.

India, too, became a favourite outlet for Burton ales. Very soon Burton's India Pale Ale became famous throughout the world. It is said that the first experimental brew was produced by Allsopp's experienced maltster Job Goodhead in – of all inappropriate containers – a teapot.

Even when, in the early nineteenth century, the Russian government put such high taxes on English ale that the sale of ale to Russia ceased almost entirely, the name of Burton as a beer-brewing centre was so well established that it had little effect on the town's trade.

Exact profits were not always declared but a brewery was not doing well if the gross final profits did not exceed 10 per cent. Thus

in 1818 James Walsh of the Imperial Brewery, Battersea, showed
that on a turnover of £246,250 the brewery had made a final
profit for the year of £20,691.

Many profits were much higher and as the breweries were still
very much family businesses, the profits tended to remain in the
same family, to be handed down from father to son, to be invested
and spread about the financial world, so that as time went by brewing families became rich and powerful.

Towards the end of the nineteenth century the number of breweries began to decline. The peak was reached around 1870, when
the huge number of 133,840 breweries were licensed. Many of
these were private breweries : innkeepers who brewed a small
number of barrels for local consumption, or farmers and even
householders who liked to turn out their own beer along with their
home-made jam and elderberry wine. To be a 'brewer' then, one
only needed a forty-shilling licence.

Gladstone's 1880 Licensing Act, with its insistence on expertise
and experience, made it almost impossible for the amateur brewers
to compete. At the same time brewing equipment became more
complex and more expensive. The day of the technical man was
approaching. Only large firms had sufficient capital to buy the
necessary equipment.

A series of appalling harvests, followed in 1887 by the Truck
Amendment Act, which forbade free beer to be included in the
farm labourers' wages and thus effectively stopped farm brewing,
brought a virtual end to private brewing.

As a result, by 1894 there were only 9,664 brewers left. Of
these, the majority were small firms producing under 1,000 barrels
a year. The number of breweries continued to diminish as more
and more of the smaller concerns found it impossible to compete or
were bought up. By 1906 the number had dropped to 1,418. But at
the same time the ones who remained became larger and wealthier.
Many turned themselves into public companies, and the practice
of buying up smaller companies increased. By 1936 there were only
453 breweries left.

The unsuccessful attempt by Charles Clore in 1959 to take over
Watneys alerted the brewing industry to its vulnerability in this
field and precipitated a series of mergers between a number of
breweries in the interests of self-preservation. Thus, when the

Monopolies Commission published its report on the industry in 1969, it showed that in 1967 there were seven large producers of beer accounting for 73 per cent of the industry's production. These seven, in order of production, were Bass Charrington, Allied Breweries, Whitbread, Watney Mann, Scottish and Newcastle Breweries, Courage, Barclay and Simonds, and Guinness. The remaining 27 per cent was accounted for by 104 brewery companies.

Since the 1960s the 'move to mergers' has lessened considerably and, although take-over rumours ripple across the floor of the Stock Exchange from time to time, there are today about eighty-eight brewery companies and groups, owning some 160 breweries and producing a variety of some 1,500 different kinds of beer. It seems likely, judging from the fierce independence of many of the smaller breweries, that what has become a fairly stabilized pattern will be with us for many years to come. But the number of home brewers is again increasing. For in fact, like tobacco, anybody can make beer. There is no law against it as long as none of it is either sold or given away. 'Beer kits', which enable the layman to make his own brew, are currently enjoying enormous popularity and this trend will probably continue.

Chapter Seventeen

It is all very well making, advertising and selling beer but it has to be carried first to the customer and then to his mouth.

For many centuries the wooden barrel or cask was the standard and only way of transporting and storing beer in bulk. The best barrels are made from oak; and the wood was plentiful in Saxon and medieval Britain.

The coopers who made the barrels were craftsmen of great power and knowledge. The oak first had to be split into staves. These were then heated over furnaces and forced into shape with the help of heavy iron clamps. Iron bands of varying length encircled the barrels to keep them in shape. The barrels had to be kept clean and constantly washed out, for if stale beer were allowed to remain in the barrel it would impregnate the wood. The barrel would have a musty smell and contaminate any new brew poured into it. A good barrel could last anything from fifteen to twenty years.

When English oak became scarce other oaks were used. Particularly popular up to 1939 was the American or Russian white oak. When these imported oaks also became scarce, brewers turned with varying degrees of success to other woods. Wood has always had a maturing and stabilizing effect on alcohol, and the taste can be altered subtly by the effect of the wooden container. 'Maturing in the wood' is a phrase in common use.

The barrel, by its very shape, has always been easy to push along, to stack in the holds of vessels, to hoist up into storehouses or to lower into cellars. Here, in cool, semi-religious obscurity, barrels, covered with damp cloths, undisturbed and remote, could remain until required.

As long as wood was cheap and the number of experienced

coopers plentiful, the trade flourished. But when wood became expensive and new materials available, brewers turned to other types of barrel. Today much of the beer is carried in metal containers, or even in huge tanker lorries.

These new methods have brought their own critics, not only amongst the traditionalists who hate to see an old custom vanish, but among the perfectionists who declare that beer conveyed in a metal container does not mature in the same way and is therefore not as good. It is true that a metal barrel adds slightly to the acidity of beer, but this can be easily rectified. Much of the beer carried in wood was already in contact with metal for, as barrels became more expensive, brewers lined them with metal so that they would last longer.

A *perfect* wooden barrel is probably still the finest container for beer; but how many barrels are perfect? Older people with memories of public houses where the beer was sucked up by a pump from the barrel below will have mixed memories. An indolent publican, uncaring for the state of his beer, and too lazy to keep his barrels clean and in good condition, would serve beer with a decidedly musty, even rancid taste. A good publican, on the other hand, conscientiously tending and nursing his barrels, could and did get a reputation for supplying excellent beer.

There was, and probably still is, an inn at Llan Ffestiniog in Merioneth called the *Pengwern Arms* which had the reputation, because of the publican's care, of having the best beer in the neighbourhood. Customers would drive into the village by bus from the slate quarry town of Blaenau Ffestiniog, they would come up the steep road from the Vale of Maentwrog or cross the mountains from Puentos Voellas, just to drink the *Pengwern* beer.

Perhaps, with the standardization brought in by metal containers, special reputations of this kind can no longer be achieved, but on the other hand, the traveller is spared the sometimes appalling sour beer that could be served up.

In Saxon and medieval days ale would be carried from the barrel in an oaken bucket with a leather thong. Sometimes the bucket would be replaced by a leather 'bottel'. Bottles were made of leather for many centuries, and are of course still made in this way in many countries, particularly by shepherds and nomads in remoter regions. Sometimes two bottles would be strung together and slung over the shoulder for easier conveyance. Chaucer's thirstier pilgrims undoubtedly carried their ale this way. The Romans had introduced glass bottles to Britain during the occupation, but the art of making glass disappeared with their departure.

For over a thousand years the earthenware jar or the leather 'bottel' remained the standard method of carrying small quantities of ale to the table. It was not until the seventeenth century that the art of making glass bottles was rediscovered. The first of the new bottles were irregular in shape. They depended very much on the expertise, whim and mood of the glass-blowers. They were small and short, with long and often rather crooked necks, and were coloured in order to protect the ale from the sun. Sometimes they were further protected by wicker-work. There was a small round depression immediately below the shoulder of the bottle for the wax seal, which showed the date of the brew and the initials of the brewer or supplier. The neck would be stopped with a cork.

With the coming of the Industrial Revolution , the individually-made bottles gave place to the mass-produced. Because machinery was rigid, bottles became standardized. Jigs were made to suit the varing requirements, and thousands of bottles, all exactly alike, were produced. The cork was replaced by the metal bottle-top.

Latterly, with glass becoming more and more expensive, many firms have turned to cans. Canned beer was popular in the United States before it became accepted in the United Kingdom. Its cheapness to produce and ability to travel well has now made it increasingly popular. The easy ring-top opening (so useful once for feeding parking meters) makes it an ideal companion for a stroll or picnic. It can be stored in the smallest of refrigerators and carried in the lightest of packs.

Plastic is also insinuating its flabby way into the bottle trade. Already plastic stoppers have made their appearance. We are now promised, as with milk, soft plastic beer containers.

The first drinking vessels were shells picked up on the seashore. The next, oddly enough, were skulls, either of small animals or, better still, a much hated enemy. The habit of drinking out of skulls continued long after many other primitive habits had vanished. Both the Celts and later the Saxons drank their ale or mead out of skulls of their enemies, killed in battle. A 'scole' was the name given to a bowl that looked like a human skull cut in half. To this day, *sköl* is a Danish form of greeting before drinking.

The horns of stags and even cattle often formed the basis of a drinking vessel. Many were polished and provided with a leather thong, so that they could be slung over a shoulder and carried. Wood and leather were extensively used. Wood, particularly oak, was carved and polished to beautiful shapes. It was reserved more for the formal occasion. Leather, being lighter and more supple, was like the horn which it began to replace, part of a person's travelling equipment, or used daily in the house.

A curious kind of cup was the Anglo-Saxon 'tumbler', so called because it could not stand up. Tumblers were either fluted or squat, but all had one thing in common : the oval bottom that meant they could only lie on their sides when not held. This was to oblige the imbiber, as if he needed encouragement, to finish his drinking in one go. A twisted pattern tumbler of this kind is mentioned in *Beowulf*.

Many were thoughtfully buried, along with ornamental ale-buckets, in Anglo-Saxon graves, so that the departed warriors could be suitably provided with the wherewithal to quench their enormous and continuing thirsts on arriving at last in the ale-flowing Halls of Woden.

The tankard made its appearance in the Middle Ages. Its first use was not for carrying intoxicating liquor, but water. The first tankards were in fact three-gallon vessels full of fresh water. They were carried by tankard bearers and supplied town dwellers, too far from fresh water sources, with the drinking and cooking water they needed. They were often made of metal; but when their use was extended to include ordinary drinking vessels, they shrank in size; and, because metal was so scarce, began to be made of pewter.

The Dutch had introduced pewter to this country in the fifteenth century. In 1482 the Pewterers were incorporated into the City of London, and given the status of a guild. Its members became freemen of the City.

Pewter tankards became extremely popular and were often elaborately and finely decorated. A seventeenth-century descendant of the pewter tankard was the 'Greybeard', a beer-jug made of pottery. It had a face with the large square 'cathedral beard' of a priest. Sometimes it was called a 'Bellarmine', so named after the Jesuit Cardinal Bellarmine who travelled around the Low

Countries at the time of the Reformation, preaching against the new religion. The Reformed Dutch potters of Delft responded by fashioning jugs that looked exactly like him, and then spending riotous and irreverent evenings drinking, like their more primitive ancestors, out of the skull of their enemy.

The Greybeard gave place in the eighteenth century to the Toby jug, which usually represented a stout old man in a three-cornered hat, seated with his pipe and jug on a bench. It was usually highly and often crudely coloured. It had a handle and one drank through the old boy's hat. Sometimes political or other celebrated figures replaced the traditional Toby. A simpler version of the Toby jug was the little brown ale-jug, that inspired the drinking song 'Little Brown Jug'.

Joke mugs were very popular. Some had holes bored into them, so that it was impossible to drink out of them without spilling the ale; others quietly poured the whole content of the mug over the drinker.

Then there were 'fuddling cups'. These consisted of three or four cups cemented together and all full of beer. The drinker was asked to drain any one of the cups. This he tried carefully to do. What he did not know was that holes were bored in each of the cups, so that as he drank out of one of them, the other three continually filled it up. The 'whistle cup' contained a whistle in its handle. When the drinker had drained the last drop, he blew sharply on the handle.

'Mazers' were so called because they were made of maple, or *masarm* in Old English. They were flat bowls with a short foot. The rim was often edged with silver, and the shallow outer surface elaborately decorated.

The 'black-jack' was a popular drinking vessel for many years, and could be found in every inn and hostelry in the country. It was a large pitcher made of a single piece of leather, twisted round and held together with stitches. Another piece of leather, this time circular, was stitched at the bottom. A leather handle and, sometimes but not always, a spout, completed the vessel. The interior was often coated with pitch so that the ale would not run out through the stitching. Black-jacks looked like those old-fashioned riding boots which came well up above the knee and were called jack-boots; hence the name. French travellers to Britain brought back to their own country strange tales of a land where men drank out of boots. The *Black Jack* was a popular name for an inn.

A super-large black-jack was called a bombard, because it looked like the short, thick, large-mouthed cannon of that name. Shakespeare describes Falstaff as 'that huge bombard of sack', while a man who could drink a bombard of ale was proud to be known among his admiring friends as a bombard-man.

The names of other drinking vessels read off like a list of strange incantations. There were naggins, whiskins and piggins, creuzes and kannes. Every district had its special name for its special kind of drinking vessel. There were also vessels without names and special vessels such as 'Margaret of Voldemar's cup'. Margaret was a Danish queen who was known for her numerous love affairs. She had a large drinking cup made with ten lips, each lip inscribed with the name of a special lover, and would drink eyeball to eyeball with the new lover.

Whatever the name of the vessel, the important thing was to get the precious liquid quickly and safely to the waiting mouth. Perhaps Pepys sums it up best of all when, on 4 January, 1667, he wrote in his diary : 'At night to sup, and then to cards, and last of all to have a flagon of ale and apples, drank out of a wood cup, as a Christmas draught, which made all merry.'

Chapter Eighteen

According to Pliny, writing in the first century AD, glass was originally discovered by accident near the Belus River. A number of merchants loaded with natron, a kind of sesquicarbonate of soda, encamped for the night by the river. One of them inadvertantly placed a hot cooking pot on some of the natron cakes. The heat melted the natron which, on mixing with the sand, produced glass.

Whether there is any truth in this legend cannot be ascertained, but Syrian glassmakers did use the sand of the Belus River to make their glass; and glass is basically made of soda and sand.

There is a form of glass in nature called obsidian, but the first man-made glass did indeed come from the East, particularly from Mesopotamia where once, it was believed, the Garden of Eden was located.

Throughout the greater part of its history glass has had an Oriental touch and feeling. For many centuries its manufacture was confined to Egypt and Mesopotamia. It was not, however, until about fifty years before the birth of Christ that an unknown glassmaker discovered how to blow glass, and thus manufacture for the first time all kinds of intricate containers.

More progress was made in the ensuing fifty years than in the preceding 1,500. The Romans used glass and took it with them wherever they went. Roman glass reached a quality that was not to be equalled again for another 1,500 years. The Romans invented the glass window, not to let in the light, but by means of slits to keep out the heat. Glass mosaics were used in Roman bathrooms. Roman glasses were set on the tables of the legionaries manning Hadrian's Wall or watching the turbulent Welsh from Wroxeter. It was adopted by the Britons, so snug and safe in their Roman-protected land. The manufacture not only of bottles but of glassware flourished.

But with the fall of Rome in 410, glass started to vanish from Europe. It disappeared almost at once from Britain, clinging on only in the Seine-Rhine area of Gaul (in France). With the final break-up of the Western Empire, and with the establishment of the new Roman Empire centred on Constantinople – it was to be the the capital of the world for the next thousand years – glass vanished almost entirely from western Europe.

For a while, glass was still buried in the tombs of the tribes who had overrun Europe. But even this habit died out under the influence of the Church in the eighth century.

No glass was made in Britain until Laurence Vitrearius left Normandy in the thirteenth century and set up a glassmaking works in the Surrey-Sussex Weald. He concentrated on window-glass.

It was at Dyers Cross, near the hamlet of Pickhurst, just over a mile from Chiddingford, that Vitrearius set up his furnaces; by 1240 he was making glass for Westminster Abbey. His son William, known as Le Verrir (the glazier), was the first to make glass vessels. It was due to his efforts that Chiddingford received a Royal Charter in 1300.

Yet though glass continued to be made in the Chiddingford area for centuries, most of it was still window-glass. The few glass vessels produced were strictly utilitarian, and it is doubtful whether any would have been used for ale-drinking. The leather gourds and wooden bowls would have seemed much more practical in that rough age.

It was not until the second half of the sixteenth century that more sophisticated and experienced glassmakers arrived from the Continent; mainly in the form of refugees fleeing persecution or poverty. These included both Protestants, from the Lorraine, and Catholics from Venice.

Carré, the great glassmaker from the Lorraine, was the first to move away from the Chiddingford area. He set up furnaces at Alford in Surrey, and finally established a glassmaking factory in London itself. Here he started making, in about 1567, quality *cristallo* drinking vessels. These were the first home-made, as opposed to imported, drinking glasses on the market.

Verzelini took over from Carré on the latter's death in 1572. He had to face stiff opposition from the London importers of foreign glass, so stiff indeed that in September 1575 his glass factory at Crutched Friars was put out of action by a mysterious fire. Verzelini was convinced that it was arson. He appealed to the Privy Council for protection and as a result, despite the protestations of the glass importers, obtained a royal licence to produce Venetian glass for twenty-one years. At the same time the importation of foreign glass was forbidden. This gave the English-based glassmakers, who had now spread as far north as Newcastle-upon-Tyne, the chance to work in peace and improve their techniques.

These early glass vessels were mostly tinted. The colour varied from blue to green, and the shades themselves differed according to the thickness and texture of the glass. They still formed only a relatively small part of the requirements of a household.

It was not until the following century when Mansell, a financier and not a glassmaker, put the glassmaking business on a national monopolistic basis, that the home production of glass drinking vessels met the increasing demand. His monopoly held until the Civil War dislocated all trade in the country. After 1650 the glassmakers became once again independent craftsmen operating on their own, but the knowledge and reputation they had achieved under Mansell's monopoly was enough to keep them going.

It was Mansell who made the first specially-designed glasses for drinking beer. These were cylindrical beakers, with simple markings on them. They were rather large and heavy, and some of them had an extra piece of glass in the foot to give them more strength. They sold at between four and six shillings a dozen. The more elegant Venetian crystal beer glasses sold at between ten and twenty-four shillings a dozen. Two shillings was a lot of money to spend on a single glass in those days.

It was the Restoration in 1660 that gave the greatest impetus to the manufacture of glass. England, because of the dislocation of the Civil War, had fallen far behind the Continent. But due chiefly to a charter given to the Glass Sellers' Company and the interest of George Villiers, second Duke of Buckingham, the glass industry developed at great speed after 1660.

By the end of the seventeenth century, forty-six firms out of a total of eighty-eight glass manufacturers were making drinking vessels, and by the beginning of the eighteenth century glassmaking reached new heights with the appearance of the rose-decorated Jacobite glass.

A type of glass made specifically for beer drinkers now appeared; it was called the rummer, and was a heavy glass with a short stem and thick base. Sometimes the bowl would be decorated with a hop and barley motif. Square-based rummers appeared about 1765, and this style of glass continued to be manufactured until the middle of the nineteenth century, their form and style of decoration changing little over the period.

Glasses grew lighter as the century progressed. This was partly due to the Glass Excise Act passed in 1745-6 whereby glass was taxed by the weight. Emphasis was then placed on decoration. Ingenious methods of producing spirals, either by using trapped air or opaque glass, were introduced in decorating the long stems.

Bowls were relatively small. There was even a dwarf ale glass, just a little over four-inches high. But then ale brews were often strong and somewhat like liqueurs.

At the same time ale was often served in posset pots, which were delicately moulded glass bowls, with one or two handles, sometimes plain and sometimes ribbed; small portions of the brew would then be transferred to the fluted glasses.

The ingredients which were put into these posset pots were sometimes rather far removed from the modern idea of a glass of beer. For example, one mixture was made in a large pan and consisted of twelve gallons of ale, twelve eggs and the gravy from eight pounds of beef. The resulting concoction was then poured into the posset pots for distribution to the guests. Some of the posset pot brews went by very strange names: Hugmatee, Knockmedown, Clamberdown and Humpty Dumpty.

Not all the glasses were small and delicate. Grog glass that had to be strong enough to take heated or mulled ale remained large and heavy. And between 1760 and 1770 at least one giant ale glass, with a tapering conical bowl, fourteen-inches tall, was produced.

With the arrival of mass production, glass lost its uniqueness. Hundreds and thousands of similar looking, utility-shaped glasses came into production. Glass became cheaper and cheaper, until it was by far the most economical way of bringing a drink, whether water, milk, spirits or beer, to the lips.

Standard pint and half-pint glasses replaced goblets, rummers and bowls. Some did have a certain individuality: the glass pint and half-pint mug remained a favourite. Special glasses were made to commemorate a specific event such as a royal wedding. Metal mugs were still, as a novelty, given a glass bottom as in earlier times; not as is generally believed so that the drinker could see anyone about to launch an attack, but in order to detect any dirt in the beer itself. Joke glasses, containing insects or frogs, were put on the market from time to time.

But on the whole, as far as the drinking of ale and beer was concerned, the standardized glass vessel became so normal, that it is difficult now to realize that a little over three hundred years ago the drinking of beer from a glass was exceptional.

Though today glass is increasing once again in price, and plastic is replacing it in many instances, particularly in vending machines, it is still holding its own where drinking ale and beer is concerned. The day may come when the local landlord dispenses the nightly litre of wallop in a plain, white, plastic mug, but at the moment the 'new-fangled' glass looks as though it's here to stay.

Chapter Nineteen

Thomas Studly, one of the first permanent settlers in Virginia in 1607, noted sadly as the ship disappeared from view on its way back to England, that in the hard inhospitable land where they were to live 'there remained neither taverne, beer house, nor place of reliefe.' Not that the home authorities forgot the requirements of the first American settlers. In the winter of that same year Captain Newport sailed from England with, among other provisions, a large consignment of beer.

Alas, most of it was drunk by the sailors on the way over.

In 1609 the Governor of Virginia asked for two brewers to be sent out; but Virginia was a low priority colony, compared with the wealth-producing sugar islands of the Caribbean to the south, and little notice was taken in London of this desperate cry. The few hundred colonists clinging on to this desolate place had to exist on water which, as an astute Spaniard of the time noted 'is contrary to the nature of the English'.

Although barley had been successfully grown in northern Virginia by Captain Weymouth in 1605, no attempt appears to have been made by the Virginian colonists to brew beer themselves. They depended entirely on the few supplies that managed to reach them from England. Much of this beer was of inferior brand, dumped by unscrupulous men on these far away colonies. One governor complained that bad 'dupper' beer had killed a number of passengers. Another noted that 'to plant a colony by water drinkers was an inexcusable errour in those who layd the first foundations. . . .' Lack of beer was considered a prime cause of much of the sickness in the colony.

More fortunate were the Dutch, Scottish and English emigrants from Delft, Southampton and Plymouth who landed on 25 Dec-

ember, 1620, further north from the *Mayflower* landing. The ship
had a supply of good beer, and although it was not enough and the
sailors again requisitioned much of it to combat scurvy that had
broken out aboard, some of it did remain for these early settlers.

Besides, the water in what was to become Plymouth, New
England, was much better than the water in Virginia. One writer
declared that New England water made people as 'healthy, fresh
and lusty as they that drink beer.'

Nevertheless, the sight of the *Mayflower* returning to England
with its supply of scurvy-fighting beer exhausted, was a sad sight
for the struggling pilgrims.

A large and better organized landing of settlers, nearly a
thousand of them, was made in 1629 on the coast of Massachusetts
to the north of Plymouth. (An advance party under John Endicott
had preceded it two years earlier.) The main party was under the
leadership of John Wintrop, a Puritan of considerable wealth and
learning. His ship, the *Arbella,* was prudently stocked with forty-
two tonnes, approximately 10,000 gallons, of beer.

The first native brewery was established soon after Wintrop's
arrival. For the next few years most of the necessary malt came
from England, but there are indications that some of the barley
used was grown locally.

Whatever the source of the malt, the brewing business
flourished. Although the Puritans were opposed to the excessive
drinking of alcohol, particularly spirits, they looked upon beer as
both nourishment and medicine. It was a vital substitute for fresh
vegetables, the lack of which had caused so many of the illnesses
among the colonists at first.

Soon, however, the sale of beer increased so much and was so
indiscriminate that regulations had to be introduced.

Taverns and inns were called 'ordinaries'. On 3 September,
1634, an order was issued by the Governor of the Massachusetts
Bay colony that ale was not to be sold for more than one penny a
quart. Six months later on 4 March, 1635, it was decreed that no
one could keep an 'ordinary' without a licence. By 1637, drunkenness had become so common that more stringent laws were introduced. Home-brewing was forbidden. All beer had to be bought
from a 'common brewer' whose output and prices could be controlled by the company.

Captain Robert Sedgwick, who was eventually to become a Major General under Cromwell, set up what was probably the first all-American brewery. It was situated at Charlestown, now a part of Greater Boston, and though its output was no doubt small, it was a definite commercial venture, and as such, was successful. But it had one disadvantage : by creating a monopoly that was not strong enough to supply all the needs of the Puritan colony, 'the weaker brethren' fell back once more to drinking brandy and spirits; so that the whole object of restricting the drinking of spirits was defeated by the very laws the Puritan leaders themselves had introduced.

In 1639, therefore, all restrictions on the production of beer were lifted. Home-brewing was once again permitted.

In the meantime, all the colonies were getting stronger. They had survived the first hard years against the Indians and the weather. Commerce flourished, particularly in Virginia, where tobacco was beginning to bring prosperity. By 1649 Virginia was reputed to have six brewhouses, had plenty of barley, grew its own hops and produced, according to a 'travel brochure' of the time, as good a beer as any found in England.

The Dutch had also turned their attention to the New World. In 1623 a small colony was established at Fort Orange (subsequently part of Albany) and another at Fort Nassau (the site of Camden, New Jersey), on the Delaware River. In 1626, after the purchase of Manhattan Island, New Amsterdam was founded.

The Dutch soon built a brewery to satisfy their well-known love of beer. Although the population hardly numbered 350, a fine brewery was set up in a street which was soon named Brouwers Stract and continued in business until 1651.

New Amsterdam evolved quickly into a small but extremely busy cosmopolitan city, the first to be established in America. Ships from many countries began to call at the port.

Inevitably, taverns began to spring up. A famous one was the *White Horse Tavern* run by a Frenchman and his wife. Another, much favoured by Long Island farmers, was owned by a Sergeant Litschoe. A third innkeeper combined his duties as mine host with those of a captain of the guard.

By 1664, when the Dutch colonies were taken over by the English, the brewers were flourishing. They continued to prosper,

the only difference being that instead of working in or around New
Amsterdam, they found their city renamed New York.

With the increase in the American population during the eighteenth century from 250,000 to a million, beer continued to be
made and drunk in increasing quantities. The Virginians were
reputed in 1724 to be very fond of Bristol beer, which was
improved by its travel across the sea; however, wine, brandy and
rum were already capturing the American taste.

Fifty years later, Filippo Mazzei, a Florentine visitor, wrote that
Americans drank 'hot punch and cold before dinner, madeira or
Spanish wine, Bordeaux in the summer – spruce beer and excellent
cider are served before wine; formerly English porter appeared
there exclusively, but it is now replaced by excellent porter made
near Philadelphia.'

Even before the War of Independence, Benjamin Franklin, who
seems to have liked beer and wine to the same degree (he hated
drunkenness: 'Drink not to elevation' he expounded) encouraged
the production of home brews. A 'Buy American' campaign
emerged as war grew nearer. In an effort to be entirely independent of English suppliers, all kinds of materials including maize,
spruce and pumpkins were used to produce beer. Pompion ale, as
ale made from pumpkins was called, never became popular, however, mainly because a slight 'tang' of the pumpkin remained, and
however patriotic one might be, this tang could not be eradicated.

When the war broke out, the Congress, meeting in Philadelphia,
appointed George Washington, who was particularly fond of
porter, Commander-in-Chief and decreed that every soldier
should have a quart of spruce beer per day if possible; cider was
also recommended.

But it is unlikely that this quota was ever fulfilled. Even in Penn-
sylvania, where William Penn once had a brewhouse erected next
to his own, beer was scarce; so scarce indeed that during the hard
winter of 1777-8 beer, along with milk and vegetables, was removed from the soldiers' diet. Nor did the English soldiers besieged
in Boston in 1776 fare any better. To add to their troubles, the
beer ran out. Urgent orders were sent to Calvert and Thrale in
London to send out 5,000 butts of strong ale.

After the War of Independence, the brewing of beer on a large
scale lapsed. There was not enough money about and the disrup-

tion of trade with England made it impossible to import alternative supplies. For the next fifty years, the brewing of beer became mainly a household occupation, with scattered small village breweries, on the lines of the old medieval English alehouses, catering for local needs.

Washington, who had been accustomed to order his beloved porter from England, had naturally, particularly when he became president, to switch over to a 'Buy American' policy. In 1789 he wrote bravely to the Marquis de Lafayette : 'I use no porter or cheese in my family, but such as is made in America : both these articles may now be purchased of an excellent quality.'

As far as the porter was concerned, he was probably thinking of Robert Hare of Philadelphia who according to Washington's secretary, Tobias Lear, produced the best porter in Philadelphia. 'Will you be so good,' he wrote to his correspondent in Philadelphia, 'as to desire Mr Hare to have if he continues to make the best porter in Philadelphia 3 gross of his best put up for Mount Vernon? as the President means to visit that place in the recess of Congress and it is probable there will be a large demand for Porter at that time.' Washington's liking for porter continued to the end of his life, even though poor Mr Hare's brewery was burnt down and America's first president had to find his favourite brew from another source.

Though men like Jefferson and Vassar were interested in brewing beer during the early part of the nineteenth century, it was not until the German immigrants began arriving in large numbers after the 1840s that the production of beer took on a new and different impetus.

The German immigrants brought with them memories of their beloved lager. For centuries the Germans had been as conscientious as their Anglo-Saxon cousins in the manufacture of beer. The difference lay in the type of beer brewed. The Germans preferred lagers, which got their name from the fact that they were kept in *lagers* or stores. The brewing of lager was carried out at a very low temperature, so that the process of fermentation was slow. A special type of yeast was used.

And here there was a problem. The slow sailing ships of the time took so long to make the journey from Europe to America that the all-important yeast was always found to be dead on arrival in the

New World. And there was no equivalent to be obtained in that continent.

How yeast eventually made its way to America has never been explained entirely satisfactorily. One theory is that with the advent of the fast Baltimore clipper ships, which cut the journey from Europe down to three weeks, some imported yeast managed to survive.

At all events, by 1840 John Wagner was producing lager beer in a small brewery at the back of his house in Philadelphia. His equipment consisted of a brewing kettle hung over an open hearth. It could produce barely eight barrels of lager at a time. The beer itself was stored in the cellar below the brewery.

It was a small beginning, but beer production was to increase dramatically. By 1844 Charles Wolf and Charles Engels had set up a brewery in Philadelphia to supply the ever-increasing German-speaking population of that town. Within a year, they were selling at the rate of 3,500 barrels.

Lager breweries appeared all over the country, particularly in New York, Pittsburgh and Chicago. Others were established in Milwaukee, Detroit and St Louis.

By the middle of the century, Philadelphia was already drinking, at 180,000 barrels a year, more lager than ale, stout and porter which, combined, accounted for 170,000. By 1861, lager was catching up ale in Illinois; while in the German-dominated Milwaukee in 1866, 68,000 barrels of lager were sold against a mere 3,600 of ale.

By the 1870s lager beer, particularly the light, bubbly, Pilsen-type beer, had become the favourite beer of the American public.

Production of all kinds of beer increased thereafter at an amazing speed. While the population of the country doubled between 1880 and 1910, the production of beer almost quadrupled: from thirteen million barrels in 1880 it reached almost sixty million in 1910.

At the same time, larger firms absorbed smaller ones. Consolidations and syndicates accumulated large funds in fewer hands. However, in 1919 there was a problem to face: Prohibition, introduced by the Volstead Act. Brewing, on a national scale, came to an end. Brewers either had to go into liquidation without compensation, or produce some product that was non-alcoholic.

Attempts were made to prove that a liquid containing 2.75 per cent alcohol could not lead to drunkenness as a man would have to drink so much of it that his stomach would not be big enough to hold it. But the law stipulated that anything over 0.5 per cent was alcoholic.

So brewers turned to other products. Some manufactured ice cream; Schlitz turned to chocolates; Valentine Blatz made industrial alcohol, which was permitted; David Stevenson Brewing Co. of New York stored furs, while Fortune Brothers Brewing Co. of Chicago did a complete volte-face and started turning out spaghetti. Many breweries closed down, or were sold at a 90 per cent loss. The Anthony and Kuhn Brewery was bought by a laundry company. It was a time of great national distress, of ingenious ways to evade the law, of bootlegging, gangsterdom, and, with the arrival of the Great Depression in 1931, misery.

But in a way the Depression helped to remove the unpopular Volstead Act. In 1933, the alcoholic content allowed under the original act was raised from 0.5 per cent to 3.2 per cent. 'Victory at last,' claimed an article in the *American Brewer,* 'and a beer bill which will make it possible to produce a good, wholesome, palatable beer! We are grateful that the will of the people finally has prevailed.'

By June of the same year, thirty-one brewers were back in business. A year later, the number rose to 756. By 1940, the sales of beer had reached pre-Prohibition levels; but there were still under half the number of breweries there used to be. Those that were in business were selling far more. The six top breweries, Anheuser-Busch, Schlitz, Pabst, Ballantine, Schaefer and Ruppert, were selling over one million barrels a year each.

War brought its problems of labour shortages as well as the difficulty of getting tin for canned beer. Malt was needed to make alcohol for munitions. Transport was difficult. But the sales of beer nevertheless increased from fifty-three million barrels in 1940 to eighty million in 1945.

After the War, an enormous expansion occurred in the production of the top breweries. Thus Anheuser-Busch's production went up from a pre-war one million to three and a half million barrels. The annual national production remained, however, at eighty million; and many smaller breweries closed down or were absorbed.

Today, American beer is putting forward a claim to be, as in early days, a universal drink. Lager, once drunk almost exclusively by the German-speaking population, is now featured as an all-American drink.

The success of the campaign depends on factors outside the control of the brewing industry, particularly the American love for soft drinks, for drug-based drinks like Coca-Cola, and for whisky.

The American adoption of beer does show very clearly that wherever Anglo-Saxons, Germans, Dutchmen or Danes may go, beer in one form or another will follow. The American pattern has been repeated in Canada and South Africa, where beer was successfully brewed at the Cape for the first time on 5 October, 1658, using locally-grown barley. In South Africa brewing remained a cottage industry until 1882 when Anders Ohlsson founded the first large-scale brewery at Newlands, Cape Province. Today there are major breweries in Johannesburg, Cape Town, Durban, Port Elizabeth, Windhoek and Swakopmund.

Beer has been adopted in New Zealand, and perhaps most spectacularly of all it has almost completely taken over Australia. In 1886, two American brothers, W. M. and R. R. Foster set off from New York for Australia. They took with them a large amount of lager brewing equipment, an engineer to install it, and, most important of all, a German-American called Sieber, who had actually learnt the art of lager-making in Germany itself, to supervise the production of the lager.

They set themselves up in a suburb of Melbourne and began producing canned lager in direct competition with the twenty breweries already installed there.

With brilliant commercial acumen, they advertised in the local papers that any hotelkeeper who stocked their lager would receive, free, as much ice to cool the lager as they needed. In the hot climate, thirsty Australian throats clamoured for ice-cool lager. Fosters' lager became Australia's most popular drink. So much so that in 1892 the other Melbourne breweries tried to get the Beer Duty Act amended and thus, by cancelling the protection given to home-brewed lager, place Foster's at a disadvantage. They were not successful.

By then however, nothing could stop the Fosters' progress. The firm had moved to larger premises. A Danish brewing expert was added to the staff, and by 1900, Fosters were beginning to export their beer – the only Australian firm to do so – to South Africa.

In 1907, Carlton and United Breweries Ltd, consisting of the six leading brewing companies in Victoria, was set up. Fosters joined the new company.

Today, Foster's can be bought in no less than twenty-eight countries. It has now established itself in the oldest beer capital of all : London. The visiting Australian pining for his native brew need no longer send for it from home, or smuggle it in in a suitcase. He can save himself a great deal of trouble and order it on the spot.

Beer has come full circle : it has encompassed the world.